NEW ASIAN
EMPERORS

THE BUSINESS STRATEGIES
OF THE OVERSEAS CHINESE

NEW ASIAN EMPERORS

THE BUSINESS STRATEGIES OF THE OVERSEAS CHINESE

GEORGE T. HALEY, USHA C. V. HALEY
AND CHIN TIONG TAN

WILEY

JOHN WILEY & SONS (ASIA) PTE. LTD.

Published in 2009 by John Wiley & Sons (Asia) Pte. Ltd.
2 Clementi Loop, #02-01, Singapore 129809

Other Wiley Editorial Offices
John Wiley & Sons, Inc., 111 River Street, Hoboken, NJ 07030, USA
John Wiley & Sons, Ltd., The Atrium, Southern Gate, Chichester,
    West Sussex PO19 8SQ, UK
John Wiley & Sons (Canada), Ltd., 5353 Dundas Street West, Suite 400,
Toronto, Ontario, M9B 6H8, Canada
John Wiley & Sons Australia Ltd., 42 McDougall Street, Milton, Queensland
4064, Australia
Wiley-VCH, Boschstrasse 12, D-69469 Weinheim, Germany

Library of Congress Cataloging-in-Publication Data
ISBN: 978-0470-82334-7

Typeset in 11/15 point Fairfield LH light by Macmillan

Printed in Singapore by Saik Wah Press Pte Ltd
10 9 8 7 6 5 4 3 2 1

This book is dedicated to our families and in memory of

James B. Haley
(1916–1988)

Dr. C. Venkatesan
(1924–1998)

Tan Thye Bee
(1914–1992)

A BOUT A DECADE AGO, and in the middle of the Asian
financial crisis, we published our first book together, *New
Asian Emperors: The Overseas Chinese, Their Strategies and
Competitive Advantages*. In that book, we questioned the assumptions foreign companies make when formulating and implementing
strategic decisions for Southeast Asia. We called the region an informational black hole, and *The Economist* (2001) labeled our book as
"important research."

Popular wisdom, and some research, has suggested that much
has changed in Southeast Asia after the crisis. We set out to determine whether our research supported these views. In the process,
we interviewed several more of the New Asian Emperors as well as
CEOs in Asia, Mexico, and the U.S. We also added new archival
data and conducted new research on the informational black hole.
We believe our findings, encapsulated in this new book, may sur-
prise you.

We conclude that important changes have occurred, but
that other authors and researchers have glossed over the changes

that we observed. The informational black hole remains, and the New Asian Emperors continue to exploit it. Simultaneously, the best of the Emperors are striving to develop the skills necessary to compete against Western companies on Western terms and in Western environments. We invite you to enter their world, and see if you can play. *Plus ça change, plus c'est la même chose.*

George T. Haley
Usha C. V. Haley
Chin Tiong Tan

ACKNOWLEDGMENTS

A BOOK OF THIS NATURE cannot be written with the interest of a day or the support of one person. We owe special thanks to the thousands of executives on whom many of our ideas have been tested and refined. In particular, the New Asian Emperors listed in the Appendix, among others, gave generously of their time, expertise, and understandings of Overseas Chinese business operations and environments so that we could interpret and project them for this book.

This book would not have been possible without the support and faith of our publishers, John Wiley & Sons. In particular, Nick Wallwork, Janis Soo and Joyce Poh of Wiley supported this project from the start, became friends over its course, and were always willing to listen, provide suggestions, and encourage us (sternly) to meet something resembling deadlines.

I would like to thank the many elderly Chinese retirees who, when I was a child in Texas, babysat with me and told me wonderful stories of the homeland they left behind and the sages who so influenced their thoughts and lives.

Finally, we owe special thanks to our families for their tolerance and sacrifice of time. Usha and I have to thank our two cats: Comet Baby, for her constant advice and unstinting support; and Marmalade, who frequently stayed up with us through the night while we wrote the book in Connecticut. Both cats loyally stood on watch to inform us when we should check for emails from Chin Tiong in Singapore! Comet Baby passed away on January 9, 2009, after giving us happiness for 17 and a half years.

Additionally, we respectfully dedicate this book to the memory of two very special people who fueled our interest in Asia: my father, James B. Haley, whose love of history and philosophy has inspired me throughout my life; and Usha's father, my father-in-law, Dr. C. Venkatesan, whose understanding of Asian business served as both guide and motivation.

George T. Haley
Deep River, Connecticut, March 2009

My father's Asian values of extraordinary hard work, controlled passion, learning, humility, devotion to his family, and sense of duty inspired and awed me. The struggles he encountered, first while managing a foreign multinational and then while starting and running his own companies in India, enlightened me; he always recounted the strife with humor and met it with intelligence, determination, and courage. I respectfully dedicate this book to my father, Dr. C. Venkatesan (Papa), a fighter to the last . . . the best of the Asian Emperors.

Usha C. V. Haley
Deep River, Connecticut, March 2009

In addition to the above, I must thank my wife Siaw Peng for her understanding and support over the years, my children, Bryan, Melvyn and Stephanie for their eagerness to see one more book by their dad on the bookshelf. Lastly, I have to thank my PA, Ms Tan Poh Ling, for her secretarial and editorial assistance on the manuscript. Respectfully, I dedicate this book to a very special New Asian Emperor, my father, Tan Thye Bee. Before his passing, his deep involvement in the family business and the Chinese networks of South East Asia provided much insights to my understanding of the various issues we discussed in the book.

Chin Tiong Tan
Singapore, March 2009

PART I

The Foundations of Understanding

CHAPTER 1

Introducing the Overseas Chinese of Southeast Asia

One generation passes away, and another generation comes; but the earth abides forever. . . . That which has been is what will be, that which is done is what will be done, and there is nothing new under the sun.

—Ecclesiastes

The epigraph summarizes the history of the Overseas Chinese and the Chinese merchant classes. The Chinese merchant classes struggled against periodic campaigns of persecution in China to gain prosperity and their dreams of a good life for their families and children; the Overseas Chinese merchants struggled against periodic campaigns of persecution in their various new homelands to gain prosperity and their dreams of a good life for their families and children; and today, the Overseas Chinese struggle against periodic campaigns of persecution in many of their present homelands to gain their dreams of prosperity and a good life for their families and children. Though our book focuses on the corporate giants and their strategic evolution, we emphasize that the great majority of the Overseas Chinese who must face the travails of their people are not the superrich of Asia but those who are still struggling and, basically, "fighting the good fight."

The Overseas Chinese, contrary to what the name would imply, do not form one people, but groups of diverse people. Like the mainland brethren they left behind, they differ by regional groupings, cultural groupings, and linguistic groupings to a much greater degree than most U.S.-born American citizens do, and almost as much physically as Americans do. Like the other great imperial populations of the latter half of the 20th century, Russia and the U.S., the Chinese people, and particularly their overseas populations, have shown great proficiency in creating and accumulating wealth when their governments permitted them to do so. This combination of courage, skills, and intelligence has created something most of the Chinese emperors of the past passionately avoided: an overseas colonial empire. The colonial empire does not constitute the traditional political empire of old but appears more akin to the economic empire that many accuse the U.S. of building. In some few instances such as Singapore and Taiwan (we will speak of Taiwan as an autonomous state although the Mainland Chinese government considers it a province), the Overseas Chinese serve as this empire's political barons; but in every instance, they dominate as the commercial emperors of this New Asian Empire. As we discuss later, despite the hardships spawned by the 1997 Asian crisis and the 2002 Severe Acute Respiratory Syndrome (SARS) crisis, most of the Overseas Chinese companies remain intact and have displayed a hearty vigor as well as adaptability in the face of external shocks.

Westerners frequently view the Chinese people as one homogeneous population, and the Chinese as always having been under the sway of an all-powerful central imperial bureaucracy until the arrival of the Europeans. Neither belief holds true. The Chinese people constitute a population of diverse religions, subcultures, and ethnic groups. Western China contains one of the earliest, and best-preserved, burial sites of a Caucasian population anywhere in the world. The local population in the region continues to manifest such physical characteristics as lighter, brown-colored hair and freckles more frequently than the norm for other Asian populations.

Frequently, the Chinese empire formed a domain in name only. Warlords from different areas would rise to challenge the center, sometimes supplanting the center. Invaders would breach Chinese defenses and create their own empires, introducing elements of their own cultures as they assimilated into the Chinese population. The center would collapse and China would break down into warring realms of various sizes and power. Frequently, the provinces would simply ignore the center's directives when they wanted to and were able to do so.

The merchant classes of the southern coastal regions would most frequently ignore the center's directives. These southern, coastal people dominated the various waves of Overseas Chinese who emigrated from China over the centuries. When the Chinese emperors periodically tried to block overseas commerce, contacts, and emigration, the southeastern Chinese provinces continued to press forward with their trading and emigration to wherever opportunities seemed to abound. In efforts to stop international trade and contacts, various Chinese emperors embarked on prohibitive measures (this is a very short and incomplete list):

- In 1424, the Ming emperor Hung-hsi banned foreign expeditions of any kind and scuttled an imperial fleet to emphasize his point.
- In 1661, the Manchu emperor K'ang-hsi banned travel and evacuated coastal regions of China to about 10 miles inland.
- In 1712, K'ang-hsi requested foreign governments to repatriate Chinese emigrants so they could be executed.
- From 1717 until his death, K'ang-hsi once again initiated a ban on travel. The emperor died in 1722, but his successors continued the ban until 1727, when they lifted it after 10 years of dismal failure.
- Not long after K'ang-hsi, European intrusions into China and Southeast Asia, and constant rebellions against the Manchu emperors by other ethnic Chinese, denied the emperors this kind of freedom of action.

- In 1959, Mao Tse-tung called on the Overseas Chinese to return home. Of the many millions of Overseas Chinese, Mao's ships picked up 100,000 seeking to come home (Hall and Kirk, 1988).

In 1911, the Overseas Chinese communities finally responded in kind to the Manchu dynasty's many punitive campaigns and policies against them and their mainland brethren: they financed Sun Yat-sen's overthrow of the Manchus. The Overseas Chinese were, and remain, the epitome of capitalistic humanity.

Patterns of Chinese Migration

The Overseas Chinese whom we discuss and who form the focus of this book are these capitalist traders. Though people generally think of the Overseas Chinese as traders, other groups also make up the Overseas Chinese communities. Wang Gungwu (1992), in his book *China and the Chinese Overseas*, discussed four patterns of Chinese migration. He identified the four patterns as:

1. The trader pattern
2. The coolie pattern
3. The sojourner pattern
4. The descent or re-migrant pattern

The trader pattern

The trader pattern represents those Chinese of commercial or professional classes who went overseas for reasons of business or employment. These people usually worked for their personal benefit or for domestic Chinese businessmen's benefit, usually but not always as relatives of some sort. If their overseas efforts met with success, more relations and associates would follow and work to expand the businesses further.

The coolie pattern

The coolie pattern represents another group of Chinese who sought their fortune overseas. These individuals usually originated from the peasant classes, or were landless laborers, or the urban poor. They went overseas on labor contracts, and many returned to China when their contracts came to an end. A large number, however, stayed to build their fortune and future in a new home. This pattern has supplied the bulk of today's Overseas Chinese population.

The sojourner pattern

The sojourners of the Overseas Chinese communities left China to act as representatives of the Chinese culture and way of life. They appeared during a time when Chinese governments were trying to reexert their control over the increasingly wealthy Overseas Chinese communities. The sojourners perceived their duty as lobbying local governments for the rights to establish Chinese schools to educate the children of local Chinese in the Chinese language and in accordance with Chinese customs. They also sought to encourage local Overseas Chinese to remain faithful to their culture and country, and importantly to their government.

The re-migrant pattern

A growing number of Overseas Chinese do not speak the Chinese language, have never set foot in China, and have even emigrated from the countries in which their ancestors originally settled. These ethnic Chinese, socially and frequently even culturally, form members of their local national societies in every way imaginable.

Though we focus primarily on those Overseas Chinese who began to build their fortunes as merchants, the greatest number of today's Overseas Chinese commercial aristocracy in Southeast Asia descended from people who fit into the coolie and sojourner patterns. Regardless of which pattern the present-day Overseas Chinese businessmen and women descended from, they are supreme business practitioners, resourceful and daring, yet rarely so daring as to be foolhardy.

Who Are the Overseas Chinese?

The bulk of Southeast Asians are, at least in part if not primarily, of Chinese origin (waves of Chinese emigration to the countries of Southeast Asia have occurred for literally thousands of years); yet generally only those people migrating to Southeast Asia in the last one or two waves of migration are considered Overseas Chinese. Most Southeast Asians considered this group to be those who arrived in their new homelands sometime in the later years of the 19th century or in the 20th century. Guangdong's and Fujian's coastal regions (to the immediate north and northeast of Hong Kong), as well as Hainan Island (between the Gulf of Tonkin and the South China Sea) dominated the last few waves of immigration. Figure 1.1 shows these coastal regions and the island. Eight primary groups of Chinese emigrated from these areas at this time (as enumerated by dialect and subdialect groupings) to the several countries of Southeast Asia:

FIGURE 1.1: *Origins in China of the Main Dialects and Subdialects of the Overseas Chinese*

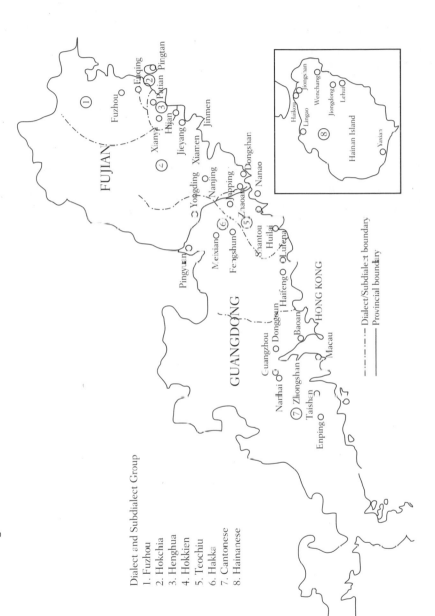

Dialect and Subdialect Group
1. Fuzhou
2. Hokchia
3. Henghua
4. Hokkien
5. Teochiu
6. Hakka
7. Cantonese
8. Hainanese

1. Fuzhou
2. Hokchia
3. Henghua
4. Hokkien
5. Teochiu
6. Hakka
7. Cantonese
8. Hainanese

When the groups left China, they tended to settle among their own people in the countries to which they went. Hence, one or two of these Chinese communities tend to dominate the Overseas Chinese populations of individual Southeast Asian countries. One

TABLE 1.1: *The Overseas Chinese in Southeast Asia*

Country	Chinese as Percentage of Total Pop.	Linguistic Groups as a Percentage of Chinese Population					
		Hok	Can	Teo	Hak	Hai	Other
Brunei	15.0	a	a	0.0	a	0.0	0.0
Cambodia	2.1[b]	2.0	10.0	77.0	3.0	8.0	0.0
Indonesia	3.1	50.0	1.5	7.5	16.5	0.0	14.5
Laos	1.0	0.0	15.0	70.0	0.0	10.0	5.0
Malaysia	23.7	31.7	21.7	12.1	21.8	7.0	3.0
Myanmar	3.0	30.0	20.0	0.0	0.0	0.0	50.0
Philippines	2.4	85.0	15.0	0.0	0.0	0.0	0.0
Singapore	76.8	40.0	18.0	23.0	9.0	7.0	3.0
Thailand	14.0	7.0	7.0	56.0	16.0	12.0	2.0
Vietnam	2.2	6.0	56.5	34.0	1.5	0.0	0.0
Taiwan	98.0	c					

Notes: *Hok = Hokkien; Can = Cantonese; Teo = Teochiu; Hak = Hakka; Hai = Hainanese.*
[a] *Although the Chinese population of Brunei is known, and it is dominated by the Hokkien. the precise breakdown is uncertain.*
[b] *For Cambodia, these are very rough estimates.*
[c] *The Taiwanese population is predominantly Hokkien and the Taiwanese dialect is considered a variant of the Hokkien dialect. Though Taiwan is not a part of Southeast Asia, it is included because of its importance to the region through cultural and economic ties.*

or two of the linguistic groups may also dominate particular trades and professions. Table 1.1 presents a breakdown of the Overseas Chinese populations of the various Southeast Asian countries. For two of them, Cambodia and Myanmar, the figures are estimates. During the Pol Pot regime in Cambodia, the Chinese, primarily city dwellers, suffered especially badly and reliable figures for their population do not exist. Myanmar has never released reliable figures on its Overseas Chinese population.

As Table 1.1 shows, the Hokkien and Teochiu people tend to dominate in most Southeast Asian countries. Historical and geographical reasons contribute to this dominance. Throughout its history, China has alternated between outward-looking expansionist regimes and inward-looking isolationist regimes. The Hokkien and Teochiu homelands lacked good farmlands but possessed relatively good ports on their coasts. Their physical distance from the historical Chinese capitals also allowed them to escape the center's notice, with the help of local authorities. Hence, under isolationist Chinese regimes that discouraged international trade and contacts, the Hokkien and Teochiu people could openly use their seafaring skills for domestic trade and fishing and had a substantial incentive to do so. Conversely, expansionist regimes that supported international trade also encouraged Hokkien and Teochiu efforts to build trading relationships. Wealth would flow into these groups' homelands through their presence in Chinese trading circles. When circumstances changed again and isolationists dominated policy, the Hokkien and Teochiu could not surrender the prosperity they had gained through trade, and they circumvented the central authorities whenever and however they could. With only subsistence farming possible, trade with other regions within China served essential needs for these groups. They used their domestic trade and shipping, and their contacts in local and central governments, to cover their activities and maintain an international trading presence. The manner in which this presence evolved had several important effects on the how the Overseas Chinese have historically conducted their business.

ADMIRAL CHENG HO

Patron Saint of Chinese Trade and Internationalism

THE MING EMPEROR YUNG-LO (reigned 1402–1424) was the last true internationalist among China's pre-communist rulers. The great admiral Cheng Ho served as the primary instrument of his international exploration, and to a limited extent maritime imperialism. Cheng Ho was a eunuch of Mongolian ancestry and a Muslim who, during Yung-lo's reign, led six great voyages (he made a total of seven). The voyages averaged two years each in length, and there are recorded visits to 30 countries, as well as Hormuz at the entrance to the Red Sea, and Jeddah on the west coast of the Arabian Peninsula.

Cheng Ho's voyages did not resemble the sailing of two or three lonely ships as the European voyages of exploration did. Rather, his were major fleets with better than 20,000 men, upwards of 60 of the largest wooden capital ships ever made, and fleets of support vessels numbering more than 200 ships. During his trips, Cheng Ho established treaties with foreign powers such as Malacca (in present day Malaysia), where he established a Chinese naval base, presented gifts to foreign rulers, and accepted tribute from them; collected many strange and exotic creatures for the Imperial Menagerie; acquired new skills; and kept an eye out for new and potentially valuable trade goods and markets that Chinese merchants could profitably exploit. He also showed the military capability and skills of the Chinese navy by defeating and capturing or killing several rulers who challenged his fleet or refused to pay tribute to his Emperor; among them were the ruler of Ceylon, whom he deported to China after settling a pretender in his place; and the ruler of Sri Vijaya (in Sumatra), who was sent to China for execution (he was a Chinese pirate who had usurped the local throne).

Cheng Ho's voyages ended on the death of Yung-lo: during his one-year reign, Yung-lo's son Hung-hsi made a clean sweep of various court factions and placed almost complete power firmly in the hands of the Confucian-dominated bureaucracy. The bureaucracy ordered all imperial records of Cheng Ho's voyages to be destroyed.

Thanks to his accomplishments, Cheng Ho is primarily viewed as having functioned in the development of trade and scholarship. Wherever you find a large number of Overseas Chinese, you will find temples and statues dedicated to this patron saint of their enterprise and vision.

In Table 1.1, the large "Other" category for Myanmar arises because the largest group of ethnic Chinese in this country originate from traditional homelands spanning the common border of Myanmar and China. The ethnic Chinese population along Myanmar's border with China has both historically lived in Myanmar and migrated across the poorly controlled border rather than emigrating from the coastal regions of China.

Table 1.2 presents the total population of the countries under consideration, together with the total Chinese populations. The table clearly reveals the substantial populations of these countries. Indonesia alone forms the fourth most populous nation on earth. The proportion of the Overseas Chinese varies from nation to nation but overall remains relatively small at just over 10 percent. Though the Overseas Chinese form a relatively small percentage of local populations, they command their local economies.

TABLE 1.2: *The Total and Chinese Populations of Southeast Asia and Taiwan*

	Total Population	Chinese Population	Percentage Chinese
Brunei	374,577	56,186	15.0
Cambodia	13,995,904	300,000[a]	2.1
Indonesia	234,693,997	7,310,000	3.1
Laos	6,521,988	200,000	3.1
Malaysia	24,821,286	5,280,000	21.3
Myanmar	47,373,958	2,000,000	4.2
Philippines	91,077,287	2,200,000	2.4
Singapore	4,553,009	3,496,711	76.8
Thailand	65,068,149	8,323,115	18.2
Vietnam	85,262,356	1,051,734	1.2
Taiwan	22,858,872	22,401,695	98.0
Total	596,601,383	51,413,830	8.6

Notes: *Figures are compiled from the U.S. Census Bureau, World Population Estimates and the CIA World Fact Book 2007.*
[a] *This is a gross estimate due to the predations during the Pol Pot era and poor records in Cambodia.*

Table 1.3 sketches the Overseas Chinese communities' economic influence in the Southeast Asian economies. As the table reveals, except in the Chinese-dominated countries the percentage of Gross National Product (GNP) generated by the Overseas Chinese in each country far outstrips the relative proportion of the population. Even in Singapore, a predominantly Chinese country, the percentage of GNP generated by the Overseas Chinese is greater than their share of the population. Historically, many people have recognized the Chinese merchant communities' energy and drive. One of Louis XV's ministers once complained that "what France needs is a touch of the Chinese spirit" (Fernandez-Armesto, 1995, p. 296).

The Overseas Chinese companies are especially important to East Asian economies. In Thailand, Malaysia, Singapore, and Taiwan, the companies and their affiliates that were listed on the stock exchanges accounted for 24.3, 24.9, 39.6 and 56.2 percent, respectively, of these exchanges' total market capitalization in 2002 (Chang, 2006).

TABLE 1.3: *Economic Participation of the Overseas Chinese in Southeast Asian Economies*

Country	Chinese as Percentage of Total Population 2002	Percentage of Gross National Product Generated by Chinese 2002
Brunei[a]	29.3	40.0
Cambodia	2.3	10.0
Indonesia	3.3	10.0
Laos	3.1	9.4
Malaysia	25.7	12.0
Myanmar	4.0	12.0
Philippines	2.8	8.4
Singapore	76.8	81.0
Thailand	11.0	33.0
Vietnam	1.5	4.5
Southeast Asia	5.3	30.0

Note: [a] *In Brunei, Chinese often do not hold citizenship, and businesses are held in partnership with local citizens.*
Source: *Table compiled from de Vienne (2004).*

De Vienne (2004) argued that those countries in which you find the largest number of Overseas Chinese generating the greatest proportion of national GNP form a direct line from Southern China to the Indian Ocean. This line also represents the maritime leg of the myriad trade routes collectively called the Silk Road and suggests that this leg of the Silk Road was dominated by Chinese traders.

What Is a Network?

Most know that the Overseas Chinese operate in networks; but a common perception erroneously assumes that these networks stem exclusively from clans or families. Strachan (1976) argued that perceptions of loyalty and trust normally associated with family or kinship groups permeate business groups (such as the Overseas Chinese) in contrast to other collections of firms under common financial control. Indeed, trust constitutes the primary factor required for the formation of the networks; hence, members of a familial clan are often preferred members of networks. Granovetter (2005) stated the importance of identifying the axes of solidarity for formation of these business groups. Three other traditional foundations for Overseas Chinese networks are the localities of origin, the dialects or subdialects spoken, and the traditional guilds (though one or a few locality-based groups tend to dominate individual guilds). Increasingly, with the Overseas Chinese companies' growth; the Southeast Asian economies' enhanced complexity; the region's interconnectedness with other, global, economic regions; and more diverse and dispersed investments, simple trust is becoming the primary determinant of who is and is not a member of a network. Here is a summary of the types and bases for the development of Overseas Chinese networks:

Network Type	Basis for Network
Clan grouping	By family surname
Locality grouping	By locality of origin in China
Dialect grouping	By dialect or subdialect spoken
Guild grouping	By craft practiced
Trust grouping	By prior experience or recommendation

Ultimately, a "network" constitutes a tool. This tool builds trust, speeds decision making, facilitates high-quality decision making, builds customer satisfaction, and in the final analysis generates competitive advantages for network members. These benefits accrue whether speaking of a network comprising separate and independent companies or executives within the same firms. Ram Charan (1991, p. 49) described networks in this fashion: "Networks are designed to empower managers to talk openly, candidly, and emotionally without fear, to enrich the quality of their decisions, to test each other's motives and build trust, and to encourage them to evaluate problems from the perspective of what is right for the customer and the company rather than from narrow functional or departmental interests." He was referring to internal networks within firms, but he could just as well have been referring to the external networks of the Overseas Chinese. The Overseas Chinese networks serve several functions. They consist of independent individuals of all kinds, businessmen and women from companies with and without ownership links, government bureaucrats, professionals and academics, private investors, and just friends.

On the surface, the Overseas Chinese form classic external networks. However, the networks also display interconnectedness, derived from one of the four traditional bases for network formation listed just above, which transform them into internal networks. An individual has a place within a clan, linguistic, locality, or guild group, and also within the fifth, nontraditional trust group. Thus, the Overseas Chinese networks actually approximate external networks with some characteristics of internal networks.

Charan's categorizations of networks shed light on the Overseas Chinese networks. First, Charan stated: "Networks are designed to empower managers to talk openly, candidly, and emotionally without fear." Family (clan), friendship (locality, linguistic, or guild group), and trust form the building blocks of Overseas Chinese networks. Intense trust in the people with whom one deals enables one to communicate with them "openly, candidly, and emotionally," without fear that what one tells them will be used to one's detriment or future embarrassment. Embarrassment forms a special risk in Chinese societies, which place great emphasis on "face." Thus the networks constitute tools of empowerment for their members. The networks allow their members to discuss important information, and through this discussion generate the best possible decisions for the networks' managers and companies. As later chapters will elaborate, given Asia's business environments, informed decision making is of crucial benefit for members of the networks. In reality, strategic decisions sometimes go wrong, for both networks and non-network-based institutions such as Western multinational corporations. For example, Apple at one time dominated the personal computer industry, fought a valiant rearguard effort once IBM entered the business, but chose the wrong strategy; until Steve Jobs led Apple back to success through innovative new products, it had severe problems maintaining profitability under the old business model. General Motors, still one of the world's greatest manufacturing concerns, is struggling to maintain market share. Its U.S. market share has fallen to 24 percent (Maynard, 2007), and it is presently facing the prospect of seeking government support to avoid bankruptcy. The Overseas Chinese firms have made similar strategic mistakes.

Second, Charan argued that with respect to their members, networks exist "to enrich the quality of their decisions." This refers to the networks' ability to transmit and analyze information that considers the entire set of implications and meanings accompanying the information. Without the richness of openly available and acquirable information that managers can find in Western industrial democracies, information serves as a tremendous competitive advantage to companies operating in Asia. By depending on, and expanding, the ability to acquire information through a network, managers increase their chance of acquiring information that will resolve the business puzzles confronting them, and give them tangible advantage against competitors.

Third, Charan stated that networks exist "to test each other's motives and build trust." Both halves of this statement have crucial importance for the Overseas Chinese networks. For several reasons we consider later in the book, in regard to Chinese culture members need to test trust in the networks. Importantly, trust does not constitute a transferable asset in the Chinese culture; consequently, Chinese business relationships often do not yield personal recommendations and endorsements. If one network member vouches for an outsider, then the network will give the outsider the benefit of the doubt, but only because the endorser assumes responsibility for the outsider's trustworthiness. If the outsider fails the trust placed in him, he jeopardizes his honor as well as the honor and judgment of the individual who vouchsafed him. The endorsing member of the network will lose face and incur debt. Hence, networks' members test motives to build trust to where it can form the sole basis for substantial investment decisions.

Finally, Charan argued that for its members a network can "encourage them to evaluate problems from the perspective of what is right for the customer and the company rather than from narrow functional or departmental interests." Though Overseas Chinese networks incorporate members who own or represent independent entities, this statement still has validity when one replaces the phrase "narrow functional or departmental interests" with "narrow personal or company interests." For an Overseas Chinese network to prosper and continue, all its members participating in a particular business enterprise must benefit from it. Without such mutuality of benefit, essential mutuality of interest and trust cannot exist. The network will collapse in a frenzy of vengeance for true and imagined deceits, and in the network's firms freezing into inaction due to inability to trust their information.

Mutualities of interest and trust increase when the networks consist of groups of people who, for the most part, have common experiences and worldviews, and who have worked successfully together, preferably over an extended period. Most members also use mutuality of interest in another fashion, building a focus for activities that eliminate the need to recheck constantly what other members do in joint projects. This lax surveillance constitutes both a strength and a weakness. However trusted an individual and consistent his or her past behavior, potential gains or costs may tempt the person to break with network partners or to break faith. Because of the high level of implicit trust, the members can initially break faith without being easily detected.

High costs can accrue to such breach of faith, especially if not detected quickly. An example came to light on June 25, 1997, when Thailand's newly appointed finance minister, Thanong Bidaya, went to the Thai central bank with his top three aides and demanded to see its financial records. The collapse of the Thai baht occurred seven days later, when the Thai government was forced to unpeg the baht from the U.S. dollar (Nanto, 1998).

Prior to the crisis, the Thai Finance Ministry had guaranteed the Thai banks and financial institutions' financial creditworthiness. As some Thai institutions' creditworthiness became suspect owing to an increasingly high level of debt to foreign lenders, the ministry reiterated guarantees to calm local markets, foreign lenders, and currency speculators. To ensure its ability to honor guarantees, the Finance Ministry requested confirmation from the Thai Central Bank on the foreign currency reserves that the bank held for the Thai government. The ministry, under Thanong's predecessor, Amnuay Viravan, could not get a response. Finally, Thailand's prime minister, Chavalit Yongchaiyudh, lost patience and appointed Thanong, president of the Thai Military Bank, as the new minister of finance.

When he took office, Thanong and his three top aides in the ministry immediately went to the currency office and personally inspected the bank's books. What they found exceeded their worst nightmares. Reported reserves should have covered almost 60 days of Thai imports; in actuality, they could cover only two days' imports. The Central Bank's chief currency trader had tied up most of its currency reserves in forward contracts. Additionally, the Central Bank had already lent more than US$8 billion to struggling Thai banks and finance companies. The largest Thai finance company, Finance One, was on the ropes and teetering badly even after having already received more than US$1.4 billion in government loans. With no more funds to lend, the Finance Ministry informed Finance One and select news media that funds had dried up. The same message went out to 15 other troubled financial institutions.

The Central Bank's officers had not reported the true state of affairs six months earlier to the government and public because the officers would have lost face. When the ministry's call for confirmation of foreign currency holdings arrived, the Central Bank's officers could not bear the embarrassment of admitting their losses, and they simply refused to respond. Once the new finance minister came and inspected the books personally, the jig was up. He transmitted his findings to the government. The revelations shattered the Thai people's confidence, as well as that of local and foreign investors, leading to collapse of the Thai economy and financial markets and eventually to the East Asian currency and financial crisis.

Although Charan adequately presented the network organization's benefits, there are important flaws in his thesis. As Charan stated (p. 52), "Companies don't build networks so that managers will 'like' or behave like 'family.'" In truth, companies don't build networks at all; *people do*. Companies can build teams, and teams can prove enormously effective management tools, but teams are not networks. Companies can also create environments to formally recognize networks and encourage them to flourish, and by so doing, use networks to accomplish the companies' goals and objectives.

In actuality, networks have always existed within companies, whether in Asia, Africa, Europe, or the Americas. There have historically been informal networks of individual executives and blue-collar employees (usually composed exclusively of one or the other type of employee). These networks generally consisted of friends and associates within the companies and most frequently formed informal communications networks that more than rivaled the companies' own formal communications networks in efficiency and influence. As the networks created informal and unrecognized structures, companies rarely used them deliberately in their plans. In fact, if the companies adopted policies that network members perceived as seriously detrimental to the interests of one, a few, or all the networks' members, the networks would frequently move to frustrate senior management plans and goals. The key elements in these networks' development, however, involved a perceived mutuality of interest, trust, and if not friendship, then some reciprocal respect. Companies cannot build networks because they cannot mandate creation of trust, friendship, or respect. As noted earlier, companies may build teams, and within teams networks may arise. However, teams cease to exist once companies decide to use team members for other projects and reassign them. Networks appear much more permanent; they continue after projects end. Networks also serve their own purposes when team members are formally working together, and beyond.

This discussion of the Overseas Chinese networks emphasizing personal trust and facilitation of transactions between limited numbers of favored individuals and companies may seem to approximate the *Godfather* trilogy of movies. However, the Overseas Chinese networks are not criminal organizations, just people who historically could rely on no one but themselves, or on no organizations or institutions but their own.

In our earlier historical discussion of the various Chinese governments' isolationist tendencies, we indicated that the networks maintained China's international trade presence; and the networks, through their contacts, knowledge, and information, frustrated the central governments' attempts to cut China off from the world entirely. The networks played a similar role in the communist era. In a different way, although the present Chinese government has a definitely internationalist orientation, the networks are playing a comparable role today.

NETWORKS IN HISTORY

A Partial List of Networks That Have Influenced Business over Time

THE OVERSEAS CHINESE NETWORKS forming the subject of this book have received much media attention and greatly influenced Southeast and East Asia's economic and business development. Yet they form only one of myriad networks. Networks have existed throughout history. We present here some prominent past- and present-day networks.

- **Overseas Indian networks.** The Overseas Indian networks are a growing force in Southeast Asia and elsewhere. They show many of the same managerial traits as the Overseas Chinese with a slightly greater tendency to depend on family members and friends as the source of their network partners. Indian networks also tend to have less diversified investments than the Overseas Chinese.

- **Hispanic *grupos*.** The Hispanic *grupos* are competent and fierce competitors. They develop through family and friendship ties. The *grupo* usually centers on a major enterprise. Growth appears diversified, but it usually follows some form of backward or forward expansion up or down a value chain. Once the *grupo* builds two or more companies of substantial size, the companies may spin off. The famous Monterrey Group of companies in Mexico represents just such a pattern among its component *grupos*.

- **The old school tie.** Though possibly losing influence, school tie networks have played a tremendous role in economic and business development in the United Kingdom and United States. Most premier university programs in the two countries offered (and still do) more than just a good education. The universities offer ways to meet and build bonds of friendship and trust with other members of society with the education, training, and mutuality of interests to advance the national economies without seriously endangering the social status quo. As education within these countries improves and becomes more generally available to the masses, and as the two countries continue to push globalization, the school tie networks have proven their effectiveness but have also become weaker within their home country.

- **Japanese inter- and intra-firm networks.** Most Western businessmen and women have heard of the inter-firm

Japanese networks, the *Keiretsu*. These organizations have proven ferocious competitors in the international arena. Despite present difficulties in the Japanese economy, the best of the nontraditional *Keiretsus*, formed around companies such as Sony, Toyota, and Honda, continue with strategies to maintain their competitive position regardless of governmental actions. Many readers may not know that several of the major Japanese companies also promote creation of class-based (*class* referring to the graduation year in which the executive was hired) networks within their managerial group. The companies encourage creation of these networks by not promoting individuals in the early years of their career, instead promoting entire classes at once. Thus, with the promotion of any one individual depending on the success of all, the individuals have an incentive to work together.

- **Criminal networks.** Criminal networks exist in all societies and countries. They have irretrievably negative effects and represent a substantial tax on legitimate businesses.
- **Secret societies.** Secret societies, influential throughout the history of the Overseas Chinese, also constitute networks and exist in all societies and nations. The Masonic Order and Magnus Dei are two particularly influential secret societies in Western countries.
- **The Greek *phylae* and *phratry*.** Greek society consisted of *phylae*, or familial clan groups, and their component parts, as well as *phratry*, or groups of allied clans. As the population of Athens grew, the city expanded its four original phylae to 10.
- **The Roman *clientela*.** A vast *clientela* ruled the West's most centrally controlled ancient empire, Rome. In the

clientela system, clients allied themselves to patrons in a pyramid of patronage, each with an influential senatorial family at the apex. The clients pledged their support for their patrons' political and military ambitions, in return for favors. At the height of the Roman Empire, these networks extended throughout Europe, Asia Minor, and North Africa.

- **Islamic clans.** The Western concept of nationhood did not exist in the early Islamic period. The early Arabian empires centered in Damascus, and later in Baghdad and Cordoba, drew on personal loyalty on the part of networks of individuals and clans, owed to increasingly fewer and more influential Islamic clans and individuals, until finally reaching the central focus of the royal family, the caliph, and a few other individuals as well as clans strong enough to challenge the caliph and his allies.

- **The feudal system.** The feudal system of Europe formed one of the most successful network systems of all time. It maintained and enhanced European civilization through difficult periods with a substantial degree of uncertainty and danger, and significant chances that European society as a whole would collapse entirely.

Source: From Haley, Haley, and Tan (2004).

Next, we discuss the role of the Overseas Chinese in Southeast Asia and the world economy. In Chapter 3, we will compare the two preeminent Oriental Asian cultures of China and Japan to understand better the origins of the Chinese business culture and see why the networks, which thwarted the central Chinese authorities' wishes, never seriously challenged Japanese central authorities.

The Role of the Overseas Chinese in Southeast Asia

As we have noted, the Overseas Chinese play a substantial economic role in Southeast Asia. This role goes significantly beyond the numbers in Table 1.3. The Overseas Chinese serve as facilitators for much of the flow of trade and investment in Southeast Asia. Through their traditionally high savings rate and financial institutions, the Overseas Chinese contribute the capital that funds investment and growth; through their distribution channels and retail institutions, they provide the goods that satisfy the needs and wants of local populations; through their philanthropy and social organizations they generate the very limited safety nets that the poor in Southeast Asia have; and through philosophical, social, and cultural organizations, transmitted for centuries through migrants from China, they have helped to render cohesion and social structures for the people of Southeast Asia to successfully withstand the onslaught of colonial cultures and maintain their cultural identity. We now proceed to consider these issues in greater detail.

The Overseas Chinese maintain one of the highest savings rates in the world. Because of their history, the Overseas Chinese believe in two basic strategies. First, they keep a significantly larger proportion of their capital in liquid form than most would consider desirable in the West. Second, they have historically believed in spreading their investments widely, making sure that the loss of any single investment will not severely damage their financial position. Their high savings generally ensure that well-managed financial institutions can withstand even the worst economic periods. Today, there are substantial concerns about the severe weakness of Asian financial institutions from Japan and China. Yet despite the problems that have beset the region over the years and decades, banks from Taiwan, Hong Kong, and Singapore have maintained their economic strength and not only survived but prospered.

Though not consistently throughout the region, the Overseas Chinese prefer to maintain control over distribution of their goods.

Perhaps this practice originates through their historical role in trade and distribution of goods; regardless of the reason, most goods sold in Southeast Asia go through the hands of Overseas Chinese intermediaries at some time in their passage between manufacturer and end user. Hence, because of the lack of market data in the region, the Overseas Chinese merchants of the region define, to a great extent, the perceived needs and wants of the region's markets.

Philanthropy is one of the basic tenets of Confucianism. Successful people have a duty to provide charitable contributions of goods, services, and cash. Throughout Southeast Asian countries, one encounters hospitals funded primarily through Chinese social organization contributions, free and subsidized food and medications distributed by Chinese merchants and associations during periods of severe economic dislocation (as happened in Indonesia during the difficulties of 1997 and 1998), and various other kinds of charitable activity. In the 1950s, Chinese societies all over Asia contributed to founding a Chinese university, Nanyang University in Singapore. Special efforts are made to relieve the suffering of the elderly, for whom the Chinese have deep respect.

As we noted previously, many waves of Chinese immigrants entered Southeast Asia over the centuries. Myriad other influences have also merged together to form local Southeast Asian cultures. If one considers the situation found in Malaysia, the truth of Southeast Asia becomes evident. The Overseas Chinese make up a substantial minority population of about 24 percent. The government and the majority of citizens consider Malaysia an Islamic country, yet the government permits the Chinese population to send their children to Chinese schools (though it does so under increasingly stringent limitations). Side-by-side with Islamic mosques, one finds Chinese and Hindu temples, and Malay, Chinese, and Indian (another substantial minority) social organizations inextricably intertwined in providing services to the Malaysian populace. The Chinese philosophical, social, and cultural organizations did not solely impart the cohesion and social structures that enabled the Southeast Asian people to withstand colonial onslaughts and maintain their cultural identities; yet they exercised at least as much influence as any other Asian culture and institution in doing so.

WU PING-CHIEN (THE GREAT OFFICIAL)

Ideal of the Chinese Merchant Class

W∪ PING-CHIEN, better known as Howqua (Chinese for the Great Official), was probably the richest man in the world during a time of true financial giants. He prospered during a period of time when the Astors and Rothschilds dominated, and Jim Bowie was the largest private land holder in the known world. During the first half of the 19th century, Howqua controlled the greatest part of all the world's trade with China. Because China would not permit importation of any bulk items from other countries, traders came to Howqua with silver and gold.

He had a reputation for scrupulous honesty and tremendous generosity. When American traders with whom he had conducted business in the past offered him promissory notes, he tore them up and reminded them that he knew them as honest men. If prices for goods he was purchasing rose after the signing of a contract, he paid the new, higher price. He fought valiantly and, in the end, futilely, to stop the British from smuggling opium into China. He paid a substantial portion of the reparations China was forced to incur after the Opium Wars—out of his own pocket, after already having paid for the improvement of Chinese fortifications before the war. He paid for a thousand and one public benefits and infrastructural improvements in Canton, his home province, and through all this, he suffered the persecution and ridicule of the Chinese bureaucracy's Confucian mandarins. The mandarins falsely charged his son with opium smuggling and gave Ping-Chien the nickname Howqua, or Great Official. The title served as a prestigious honorific for a bureaucrat, but only as mockery for Ping-Chien, a member of the merchant class (the lowest of Chinese social classes).

Ultimately, of all the great officials of China in the last century, history remembers only Howqua, the greatest of the Chinese merchants. His portraits hang in many places, including the East India Hall of Fame in Salem, Massachusetts, where one may see the portrait shown in Figure 1.2.

FIGURE 1.2: *Wu Ping-Chen (Howqua, or Great official)*

Source: This portrait of Howqua resides in the East India Hall of Fame in Salem, Massachusetts. (From Haley, Haley, and Tan, 2004).

The Role of the Overseas Chinese Worldwide

The Overseas Chinese play a large and ever-widening role in the international arena. Among the brands of Overseas Chinese companies, one finds such names as Acer Computers, the largest presence in the computer industry of any company headquartered outside the U.S. or Japan; Creative Technology, which holds dominant market share in the computer sound-card industry with its Sound Blaster brand; San Miguel Beer from the Philippines; Tiger Medical, makers of Tiger Balm; several banking concerns, such as United Overseas Bank, Overseas Chinese Banking Corporation, Hong Leong Bank, and Dao Heng Bank; hotel and resort properties, such as Shangri-La Hotels; industrial concerns such as Formosa Plastics; and even some Chinese companies engaged in overseas trading, the business that created the wealth of the great Overseas Chinese companies, such as Kuok Brothers, which at one time controlled 10 percent of the world's sugar trade, and Li & Fung.

The Overseas Chinese role in international trade, however, goes beyond the companies they personally control. The Overseas Chinese form a tremendous conduit between Western companies and the liberalizing, formerly communist countries of Asia. Through their contacts within the governments of these countries, and their networks within those countries, they frequently facilitate investments that could languish from a clash of cultures or lack of knowledge. Examples of such an occurrence happened when Daimler-Benz asked the government of Singapore to intercede on its behalf in 1996 with the government of Vietnam (Kraar and Woods, 1996), and when Coke brought Robert Kuok in as a partner in its Chinese investments to help make them profitable. In Vietnam, Daimler-Benz was stuck with a significant sunk cost in an investment that had stalled for an extended period of time. The Singaporean government, thanks to its "Singapore, Inc." self-image as middleman to the world (as described in Haley, Low, and Toh, 1996), actually constitutes one of the great

Overseas Chinese enterprises (see Tsui-Auch, 2006). Soon after that request, Singapore's Senior Minister Lee Kwan Yew visited Vietnam and got the investment back on track for Daimler-Benz.

Following Chapters

In succeeding chapters, we present a short discussion of Confucianism, its centrality to Chinese culture and life, and its impact on traditional Chinese business philosophy and practice. We then discuss how the history of the Overseas Chinese has combined with Confucianism and the environment to mold the people one meets and does business with today. In the process, we describe the present strategic decision-making environment in Asia, and its evolution. Next, we describe the decision making of the Overseas Chinese. Though many say the Overseas Chinese do no strategic planning, we explain the basic concepts and philosophy that underlie their decision making, demonstrating its similarity to well-accepted Western conceptualizations of strategic planning. We conclude by discussing the implications of the Overseas Chinese model of planning for their strategic partners (and competitors). In doing so, we present the views on strategic planning and decision making held by some of the most influential and private of the New Asian Emperors, together with those of leading members of the next generation.

CHAPTER 2

Confucianism Plus: The Philosophical and Cultural Roots of the Overseas Chinese

No one likes Confucius before they come to power. Once they do, they begin to see his good side.

—**Kong Fanyin,** a present-day descendent of Confucius

In the epigraph, Kong Fanyin spoke one of the great truisms of Asian political and business life. Confucius opposed rebellion against a legitimate prince under all circumstances. The second great sage of Confucianism, Mencius, introduced the idea that a prince can behave so improperly as to justify the masses' overthrowing their rightful prince. In either case, both great sages preferred compromise and conciliation to confrontation, just as the New Asian Emperors often do.

Twenty years ago, there were very few studies of non-Japanese Asian business groups; these studies catered to small groups of scholars actively studying Asian business practices without gaining much attention from the business community at large. However, in the last couple of decades or so, a number of studies have appeared that trace these Asian business groups' growing influence and development (for example, Chang, 2006; Hamilton, 1996; Khanna and Palepu, 1997; Redding, 1995, 1996; Akamatsu, 1998). Many of these studies have questioned the simplistic descriptions of Asian and Overseas Asian business firms that accompanied Asia's early economic development. Some recent scholars have claimed that many earlier studies err by emphasizing Confucianism; these scholars state that more modern and specifically economic philosophical systems of behavior have replaced the old traditional systems (Hamilton, 1996). Still, others (for example, Granovetter, 2005; Strachan, 1976) have argued for identifying those factors that contribute to the business groups' social structure and social solidarity, such as religion and belief systems. In this chapter, we discuss Confucian, Buddhist, and Taoist economic and behavioral principles to gain greater understanding of their implications for business practices in the region. In later chapters, we elaborate on the Overseas Chinese companies' present-day practices and demonstrate the influence of traditional philosophies on them.

A relatively unsuccessful itinerant teacher and government bureaucrat named K'ung Fu-tzu (later Latinized to Confucius) had a cosmic effect on Chinese societal and cultural development. His dramatically profound influence, and that of his greatest adherent, Mang-tsze K'o (later Latinized to Mencius, and sometimes referred to as the Second Sage), on China and the Chinese culture, though dimly recognized and often misunderstood by non-Chinese, is apparent to the New Asian Emperors. Indeed, in a 1985 speech to the World Management Congress, Robert Kuok, Malaysia's great Overseas Chinese tycoon, said, "As children, we learned about moral values—mainly Confucian."

Confucius, and especially his successor, Mencius, waged a philosophical war for the heart and soul of China's spiritual development. Their victory created a humanistic philosophy and outlook on life that believed in hard work, conservative adherence to traditional values, the dominance of society over individual and family over society, and a society in which there is a place for everyone, and everyone has his or her place and role to play in society. Though the West knows little of Mencius, who lived some 100 years after

Confucius, they know much more of Confucius through Mencius' interpretations of his writings than through anything Confucius communicated directly. One can attribute the development of Confucianism to Mencius' championing of the inherent goodness of man, something Confucius neglected to address.

As the "Plus" in this chapter's title indicates, Buddhism and Taoism represent two other strong influences, alongside Confucianism, on Chinese culture and society. These three streams of thought fused together to form the Chinese view of man's place in society and influenced Chinese character and personality development. The four men at the center of these enormously influential philosophies, the Buddha, Confucius, Mencius, and Lao Tzu, were not messengers from heaven or prophets; they were philosophers who felt they had discovered important perspectives on living good lives. Confucius and Lao Tzu were probably contemporaries in ancient China; Mencius lived in China about 100 years later; and the historians have documented well the Buddha's life in India in the fifth and fourth centuries BC. Though Westerners often think otherwise, and Taoism and Buddhism have evolved into religions, none of the four saw himself as the founder of a religion but only as a teacher of a philosophy of life, something Confucius, Mencius, and Lao Tzu referred to sparsely as "The Way." The four recognized the importance of the "heavens" in life but never defined the heavens; they merely accepted the heavens that their societies had defined.

The Overseas Chinese have cast off many of the elements within the streams of thought that historically limited Chinese economic development (Redding, 1993); however, the basic economic and behavioral tenets that flowed from these philosophies influence their business practices today. First, though they have circumscribed the limiting influences, their perceptions of the ideal in human behavior—and frequently their interpretation of other people's behavior—remain rooted in their philosophical traditions.

Second, the development of the Overseas Chinese has resulted from the creative tensions and conflicts between the influence of these philosophical schools on Chinese culture, life, and governance on the one hand, and human nature and the practical necessities and experiences of life on the other. However, these philosophies fail to incorporate the economic aspects of human nature into their tenets of behavior, presenting us with several paradoxes, and with some of the greatest differences between Western and Chinese societies.

Confucianism offers a prescription for the proper behavior of men, and especially for members of the gentlemanly classes, in their interactions with society, their peers, and their princes. (Through the balance of our examples and text on Confucianism, we use male pronouns. Confucian philosophy is inherently sexist and focused almost exclusively on the father as the central figure. This male-dominated perspective on life viewed females as subordinate to males, and it continues to do so today.) The philosophy places its entire emphasis on human behavior and man's place in society. Within Confucius' writings, some passages address natural or Godly phenomena and human nature, though he does not place them at the center of his philosophical deliberations. The central role in Confucian philosophy goes to human social interaction. This characteristic Confucian approach appears in book 5, chapter 12 of *The Analects*:

> Tzu-kung said, Our Master's views concerning culture and the outward insignia of goodness, we are permitted to hear; but about Man's nature and the ways of Heaven he will not tell us anything at all.

Buddhism and Taoism both emphasize the oneness of nature and mankind's position within that oneness; they fail to incorporate the practical, economic aspects of human nature in their prescriptions for behavior considered desirable within that oneness. Buddhism emphasizes creating an ideal of human nature, a goal people can achieve through learning and acts of will. Taoism focuses on the paradoxical duality of all nature and gaining an understanding of nature through knowledge of that duality and its implications.

Confucianism, Buddhism, and Taoism refuse to pander to mankind's inherent greed; desires for independence, success, and recognition; and preference for reacting directly to external stimuli. The philosophies acknowledge the basic, economically practical aspects of human nature, view them as undesirable, and attempt to do away with them. Conversely, philosophers with analogous influences on Western culture, thought, and behavior, from ancient Greece and the Age of Reason, recognize and incorporate human nature's underlying, economically practical aspects into their basic tenets of desirable behavior rather than reject them. Western philosophers seek to exploit the directional thrust of human nature's practical, economic aspects and focus it toward socially desirable goals such as wealth creation for society as a whole, reduction of human suffering through charitable contributions, and use of personal wealth for societal good.

There are significant differences among the Confucian, Buddhist, and Taoist approaches to mankind's economic nature. Though traditionally rejecting the more economically practical aspects of human nature, the philosophies have incorporated unique reactions to them. For example, Buddhism rejects acquisition entirely in prescribing the ideal in human behavior. Taoism, though not rejecting acquisition outright, argues through its perspective of nature's paradoxical duality that wealthy men should not acquire more but should want less. Individuals wanting less will always have sufficient means to obtain what little they want and maintain a surplus; hence such individuals will always have more wealth than the individuals wanting more, acquiring more, and never seeming to have enough while obtaining everything they want. The Overseas Chinese have altered this important perspective to their own use and benefit: they generally live frugal lives relative to their income and have a high savings rate. For example, in 1996, New Asian Emperor Li Ka-shing, with estimated assets of US$8 billion at that time, was finally persuaded by his son Victor to change his 20-year-old Mercedes for a Nissan President. In public, he wears a Citizen wristwatch that cost him US$50. During the Asian financial crisis, Robert Kuok bought a mansion on Hong Kong's Deep Water Bay Road, close to a nine-hole golf course that the New Asian Emperors frequented for early morning rounds, for the bargain price of HK$80 million. He initially lived in the house but worried that it was excessive even for a man worth several billion dollars. Finally, he razed the house, built five unpretentious town houses in its place, took one for himself and two for his family, and rented out two more. Studwell (2007) remarked that Kuok lives as a modestly successful bank manager in the U.S. would.

China's most influential philosophers' classic works form a surprisingly small body. *The Analects* of Confucius constitutes an extremely short masterpiece, readable in a few hours. Lao Tzu presented his philosophies in two books, the *Tao Ching* and the *Te Ching* (now united into the *Tao Te Ching*, or the *Book of Tao*), containing a series of very short chapters, some of them only three or four lines long. More exists of Mencius' writings, although of a limited quantity, than of either of his predecessors. Confucius' and Mencius' philosophies are presented, much as Plato's was, as conversations between the master and his students or between contemporaries, or simply as their statements.

Few scholars today seriously doubt the basic intent of Confucius' writings. Yet serious schisms in interpretation occurred in the past, the most serious during Mencius' time. That schism focused on the effects that basic beliefs about human nature would have on the interpretation of Confucian thought. Mencius championed the basic underlying goodness of mankind. He argued that, left to their own devices and inherent nature, men would develop as good beings, and that Confucian thought and philosophy should be interpreted from this perspective. He believed evil men had their inherently good nature corrupted by their environment. His two great contemporaries both held views that outraged Mencius' high moral perspective; if their philosophies had gained the upper hand, the interpretation of Confucianism, and especially of Neo-Confucianism, that later took hold, would have differed profoundly from what we see today. Confucius himself only addressed the how of things, the practical side of men's behavior and interactions with society. Confucius rarely addressed anything as nebulous and irrelevant as men's underlying nature.

Yang Chu was the first of Mencius' great contemporaries, and the one whose philosophies he most despised. Yang Chu, a Confucian, pressed the argument of extreme egoism. He argued that men had a primary moral duty to survive as long and as comfortably as possible. He did not include concepts of charity or self-sacrifice in his philosophy. Extreme and incorrect interpretations of some chapters in Lao Tzu's *Tao Te Ching*, often quite obscure, may have influenced him. For example, chapter 5, book 1, of the work uses the analogy of straw dogs or temple offerings for people; prior to the offerings, straw dogs and people were treated with great deference, but afterward, they were trampled into the ground:

> Heaven and earth are ruthless, and treat the myriad creatures as straw dogs; the sage is ruthless, and treats the people as straw dogs.
> Is not the space between heaven and earth like a bellows?
> It is empty without being exhausted:
> The more it works, the more comes out.
> Much speech leads inevitably to silence.
> Better to hold fast to the void.

If one takes heaven's behavior as the ideal, then one should behave ruthlessly, without showing charity. One should also never contribute one's all to society, whether through self-sacrifice or performance for the public good. Hence, Yang Chu's conclusion that self-sacrifice brings destruction, charity brings abuse, and the best goals involve clinging to the void that surrounds individuals, surviving as long and as well as possible, and exploiting every situation for personal gain. Yang Chu's philosophy seems remarkably similar to the famous pronouncement of Michael Douglas's character in the movie *Wall Street*: "Greed is good!"

Yang Chu's philosophy had little influence on Mencius' Confucian economic philosophy. However, there are immense similarities between the economic philosophy of Confucius and Mencius and that of socialism. Thus, for Asia's communist countries unlike for the Soviet Union, socialism did not constitute the short-term grafting of a foreign ideology onto society. To a great extent, socialism reestablished traditional economic philosophies that dominated the region, except during the short hiatus of Sun Yat Sen's Chinese Republic. The communist system often used new names for old concepts. Hence, the assumption that Asian communist governments and parties will suffer the same, almost overnight, collapse that communist governments suffered in the Soviet Union and Eastern Europe appears mistaken.

Mo Tzu, a charismatic philosopher and leader, was the second of Mencius' great antagonists; his movement collapsed soon after his death. Mo Tzu led a universal love movement, surprisingly similar to the one experienced in the West in the 1960s. He argued that humankind's greatest duty involved living life to promote free exchange of love, and treating all countries as one's own. Mo Tzu, like the universal love advocates of the 1960s, advocated extreme pacifism. Mencius scorned Mo Tzu's philosophy; he felt that universal love removed the family from the center of men's lives and would require that men not love and honor their own fathers above all other people.

THE BUDDHA

Prince Among Saints, Saint Among Princes

THE BUDDHA WAS BORN AROUND 566 BC into a princely Hindu family that ruled from its capital city, Kapilavastu; he died around 483 BC. His true name was Siddhartha. He enjoyed a traditional upbringing, and the first 29 years of his life appear entirely unremarkable. But he then abandoned his home and family, including his wife and newborn son, and embarked on a life as a wandering ascetic. For several years, he tried many of the traditional activities undertaken by Indian ascetics, including various penances as well as programs of austerity and self-denial, and came away disappointed and unenlightened. With this initial failure, he turned to meditation. His still famous seven-week period of meditation under the Bo tree had better results. He came away enlightened and with his philosophy firmly developed.

He concluded that all unhappiness and suffering were rooted in desires, which were in turn rooted in ignorance; the true path to *Nirvana*, or salvation, lay in mastering and conquering desires. He taught that as one progressed through rebirths, the soul's success in reaching *Nirvana* came through practicing the Noble Eightfold Path: Right Aspirations, Right Conduct, Right Effort, Right Livelihood, Right Meditation, Right Mindfulness, Right Speech, and Right Views. Once he established his philosophy and teachings, he reverted to an itinerant ascetic, now preaching his philosophy, and the people who listened to his teachings called him the Buddha, or the Enlightened One.

From the time of his enlightenment to his death, the Buddha traversed northern India, spreading his message and founding orders of monks and nuns. His new orders originated as mendicants, but over time they formed monasteries, formalized the Buddha's teachings and philosophy, and founded the first great centers of learning in India to promulgate the Buddha's philosophy to the public. Rather than the founder of a new religion, the Buddha viewed himself as a Hindu reformer. He championed many revolutionary reforms, creating orders of nuns and rejecting the caste system, which had become increasingly rigid and oppressive with the Brahmin caste domination of traditional Hinduism. The Mauryan Emperor, Ashoka, became one of the new philosophy's greatest converts; he sent out its early missionaries to spread Buddhism into China and Southeast Asia, thereby ensuring its survival, success, and influence.

Confucius never lived to see his great influence, but Mencius did. Mencius vanquished his philosophical opponents and observed the triumph of his philosophy of Confucian humanism and human nature's essential goodness. Though Mencius enjoyed limited success in his political career, he collected sufficient wealth through serving his Chinese princes to retire to a life surrounded by students and preparing his great works for publication. Confucius, on the other hand, died as he had lived, an itinerant teacher, philosopher, and government bureaucrat. His students worshipped him, and other thinkers and educated people respected and esteemed him; but the Chinese princes of his day failed to champion him.

Confucianism's Influence on Chinese Trade and Economics

Confucianism's most apparent influence on Chinese economic culture deals with perceptions of the merchant classes and profit motives:

Confucianism frowned on both. The Confucian philosophers viewed the mobile, merchant classes with suspicion and considered them the lowest class of humanity. Instead, the philosophers exalted peasants who were tied to the land. The Chinese peasantry, though immobile, did not approximate Russian serfs or Spanish peons; their attachment to the land arose because their income originated from their work on the soil. This inability to transfer livelihood meant that the government could locate peasants to tax them, draft them into work projects, and use them to fill the ranks of the army. The peasants' livelihood depended on their staying in known locations and on the government's ability to provide the peasants with a safe, stable environment at those specific locations. In so doing, and with the peasants' taxes supporting the bureaucracy and army, Confucian philosophers viewed the peasants and the government as having synergistic interests. In short, the government could easily control the peasants because they lacked mobility and needed the government's services.

The Confucian perspective on society also contributed to their philosophers' perceptions on the inherent controllability of the peasantry. The philosophers envisioned appropriate places and roles for everyone in society, and they saw these roles as good for individuals and society. Mencius taught this philosophy as the basis for good rule:

> There are affairs of great men, and there are affairs of small men. Moreover, it is necessary for each man to use the products of all the hundred crafts. If everyone must make anything he uses, the Empire will be led along the path of constant toil. Hence, it is said, "There are those who use their minds and there are those who use their muscles. The former rule; the latter are ruled. Those who rule are supported by those who are ruled" (Lau, 1995, p. 62).

This idea that rulers must control small men runs throughout Confucian philosophy. This emphasis on control of the lesser by the greater introduces acceptance of authoritarianism into the Chinese mind-set, which Western managers or political figures rarely find among their subordinates. Li Ka-shing projects more benign patri-archy when he often refers to himself in public as "the friendly lion." But operationally, many traditional Overseas Chinese com-panies that retain Confucian practices are encountering problems recruiting professional managers. Few bright young managers want to work for a company that will never give them a role in formu-lating corporate strategies because of their age or lack of kinship or friendship ties. In Overseas Chinese firms, whether traditional or professionally managed, respect for authority and age too often also rules out any criticism of the boss. However, importantly, Confucian superiors, or great men, had to use their authority for the benefit of small men, and to do so with as little force as pos-sible; the Confucians perceived small men, or those of the subor-dinate classes, as incapable of governing their own actions. The passage below from Mencius on this aspect of rule uses the term *gentleman*. The Confucian gentleman served as courtier in the courts of the rulers, and as an advisor and educator of the royal young. Bloodlines or force did not restrict membership; rather, membership depended on an individual's level of educational attainment and training in the social graces and in the rituals and behaviors necessary for life at court.

> Only a gentleman can have a constant heart in spite of a lack of a constant means of support. The people, on the other hand, will not have constant hearts if they are without con-stant means. Lacking constant hearts, they will go astray and fall into excesses, stopping at nothing. To punish them after they have fallen foul of the law is to set a trap for the people. How can a benevolent man in authority allow himself to set a trap for the people? (Lau, 1995, p. 60).

This statement explains the Confucian perspective on the relation-ships between individuals in authority and subordinates, as well as the Confucian economic perspective that we will now discuss.

The Confucians frowned on merchants and discriminated against them for exactly the opposite reasons for which they exalted peasants. Merchants enjoyed mobility, which contributed to their livelihood. By locating and transporting goods across locations, merchants earned their profits. However, this mobility meant the government could not depend on the merchants. Merchants could, for example, avoid military service by moving their goods and families to other locations. They could also avoid taxes by hiding earnings in neighboring territories. The merchants did not need the government's safe and stable environment for their livelihood; if the environment became too dangerous, they could move. In other words, the government could not control the merchants as completely as it did the peasants. The Confucian mandarins' perception of peasants and merchants resembled the communists' perception of workers and capitalists: they exalted and controlled the former, and they demonized and persecuted the latter.

Confucianism also viewed the profit motive as corrupt. For example, in book 4, statement 16, he said, "A gentleman takes as much trouble to discover what is right as lesser men take to discover what will pay" (Waley, 1996, p. 24). In his introduction to Waley's translation, Robert Wilkinson gave another, more damning interpretation of this passage and other related ones: "The lack of moral principle manifests itself in various forms of egotism but principally as greed: while the gentleman does what is right, the small, or lesser man only considers what is profitable." This theme runs consistently throughout Confucianism.

Neo-Confucian mandarins during the Ming and Manchu dynasties may have also viewed the merchant classes as a potential threat to their power. Mencius' statement quoted above damned the merchants from two perspectives. First, the government could not depend on independent merchants to "support those who rule." Second, merchants primarily used their mind, not their muscles; because the merchants could also provide small men with the goods necessary to pacify them, one could argue that the merchants should rule, not the mandarins and their princes.

CONFUCIUS

Master K'ung

CONFUCIUS IS TRADITIONALLY CONSIDERED to have been born in 551 BC, in the state of Lu during the Zhou dynasty, and to have died in 479 BC. His father died in Confucius' infancy and his mother raised him.

He encountered severe constraints and poverty due to his life situation. He seemed to have early success in his career, obtaining modest public offices within the bureaucracy that could have potentially offered him a position of influence before he retired. Unfortunately, the Zhou dynasty was in serious decline during Confucius' time, and the constant ebb and flow of the political situation served to disrupt his career and aspirations. His home state of Lu was lost to the empire when three influential and wealthy merchant families joined together to wrest control of the state away from the center. As the provincial officer responsible for maintaining order, Confucius failed to rein in the rebellious families and was disgraced.

Once his career as a mandarin bureaucrat stalled, he lived as an itinerant teacher and bureaucrat in search of his next posting. During the Confucian era, bureaucrats could travel from state to state in search of employment. At one time, in desperation, Confucius considered leaving China to seek service in barbarian countries. His difficulties and apparent frustration in gaining material success in his civilized homeland may have led to three traits in Confucian philosophy. First, and most important, he exhibited open disdain for personal gains or profit, something he argued that the true gentleman never sought; second, he expressed dissatisfaction with civilized society and idealized the "noble savage"; and finally, Confucianism was an authoritarian philosophy, arguing that the ruled should never challenge the rulers.

The Analects (in Chinese, the *Lun Yu*) forms the primary body of his philosophy that has survived to modern times. The English translation of *Lun Yu* (*Selected Sayings*) serves as the most accurate description of the masterpiece, basically a collection of sayings rather than a coherent text. The power of Confucian thought serves as a tribute to the discerning scholars who interpreted his sayings over the years as much as to Confucius' wisdom and understanding. Though many view his philosophy as lofty, Confucius addressed the practical aspects of day-to-day living almost exclusively. His great appeal today may stem from his being the most human of "great officials," and the Great Official of all humanists.

Mencius indirectly acknowledged the merchants' importance as those who arranged for the exchanges necessary for "one man to use the products of all the hundred crafts." The merchants also often had financial strength. Thus, they would have represented a substantial, legitimate threat to the mandarins.

Confucianism emphasized the ability to control as it rejected loyalty to the government for patriotic reasons; it opposed the strong patriotism that has caused such tremendous pain and suffering in more modern times. To Confucius and his followers, families rather than states constituted the basis for society; the duty owed by sons to their fathers assumed primary importance, and for gentlemen the duty owed to proper social conduct, or to following the Way, assumed dominance. Duty to the state that conflicted with duty to father and family became immoral, and the latter prevailed ethically. Consequently, Confucius argued in book 13, statement 18:

> The Duke of She addressed Master K'ung, saying: In my country, there was a man called Upright Kung. His father appropriated a sheep, and Kung bore witness against him. Master K'ung said: In my country, the upright men are of quite another sort. A father will screen a son and a son his father— which incidentally does involve a sort of uprightness.

An old Chinese proverb reflects this important Confucian belief of moral duty and loyalty by stating, "A man cannot be a good patriot and a good son." This is an important factor because it begins to explain the concept of moral duty and loyalty as they are understood by Confucianism. Though Confucian ethical and moral standards are rightfully held in high esteem by many Westerners who abhor the relativist nature of some Western philosophical schools, Confucianism is in fact a contextual philosophy that, in some of its effects, resembles relativism.

According to the Confucians, mankind's other primary duty involved maintaining proper place and behavior in society. This view did not translate to prohibition against personal advancement or a demand for a static society. Confucians believed that men should strive to advance themselves as much as possible, so long as they maintained all the proper ritual behaviors for each stage of life progression. Confucius viewed the strictures and requirements of the Way as the governor of gentlemen's actions. In book 8, chapter 13 of *The Analects*, Confucius elaborates on the strictures of the Confucian code:

> The Master said: Be of unwavering good faith, love learning, if attacked, be ready to die for the good way. Do not enter a state that pursues dangerous courses, or stay in one where the people have rebelled. When the Way prevails under Heaven, then show yourself; when it does not prevail, then hide. . . .

As the quote indicates, Confucius did not consider patriotism a virtue. "My country, right or wrong!" certainly did not constitute the gentleman's battle cry. The gentleman vowed loyalty not to his country but to the Way. When a prince pursued "dangerous courses" (or policies obstructing proper observance of the Way or maintenance of social order), Confucius recommended that the gentleman desert his post and leave for a better-run state—advice that Confucius himself followed more than once! Consequently, many New Asian Emperors, indoctrinated in the Confucian way, do not expect loyalty and demand constant reassurance of it from their employees. Canning K. N. Fok, who serves as chairman of the board of directors of Hutchison Whampoa, receives an annual pay package of about US$15 million, among the highest salaries in Hong Kong for professional managers. He has overseen the investment of more than $25 billion in Hutchison's third-generation mobile telephony business. Yet his pay and authority came with certain demands from his boss, Li Ka-shing. A former employee stated: "If you work for Li, you have got to keep showing your loyalty all the time." Fok rarely sleeps before 2:00 a.m. and checks into the office at regular hours for Li. Similarly, Colin Lam serves as the right-hand man for Lee Shau-Kee, Li's biggest rival in Hong Kong; Lam owns an enormous house on Repulse Bay, but spends most nights at his flat on May Road on the other side of Hong Kong. He does this for physical proximity to his boss, who may summon him at any time.

According to Confucian economic and social theory, a key part of good rule involved supplying a sufficient degree of wealth to all small men so that they could provide themselves and their family with basic necessities. This perspective, combined with Confucian distaste for the profit motive and Taoist economic philosophy discussed earlier, lays the foundation for traditional Chinese economic principles followed by rulers for centuries. Unlike Western economic philosophy, Chinese traditional economics pursues maintenance of a minimally acceptable subsistence level, not wealth, for all small men. The excess over and above that subsistence level yielded earned benefits for the greater men of society who promoted good rule. Chapter 3 of book 1 of the *Tao Te Ching* elaborates this Taoist principle:

> Not to honor men of worth will keep the people from contention; not to value goods which are hard to come by will keep them from theft; not to display what is desirable will keep them from being unsettled of mind.

Chinese traditional economics suffocated the goal of wealth creation, which meant displaying desirable goods, valuing rare goods, and in short, allowing greater wealth and concomitant honor to create "contention among the people," a situation good government sought to prevent. Consequently, Confucian principles and traditional Chinese law forbade merchants from wearing fine clothes outside the home and riding horses or wagons. Merchants had to walk everywhere; thus the mandarins intended to show that merchants were no better than other small or lesser men.

The Family

The family is an overwhelming constant in Confucianism. The family dominates the individual's moral considerations and behavior. The family sets the tone for the individual's relationship with others whom he meets daily, for the individuals' relationship with the sovereign or other authority figures outside the family circle, and for the individual's relationship with society in general. Confucianism offers an immediate and unending perspective on the family: individuals owe responsibility to their nuclear and extended families, especially to their parents, and also to their ancestors. Consequently, the mention of economic sufficiency referred to sufficient income to house, clothe, and feed living family members, and to make appropriate offerings and conduct rituals for dead ancestors.

A Confucian's often paternalistic, management style permeates the ranks of the New Asian Emperors, and fathers often assume the role of professional boss vis-à-vis their children. Ng Teng Fong, Singapore's biggest private landlord, offers a glimpse into this style. His eldest son, Robert, runs Sino Land, his family's business in Hong Kong and one of the top developers in the territory. Robert, educated at an English boarding school and in his 50s, lives in an apartment rented from the company; he owns only about US$1 million of Sino Land's equity. His father telephones every day to check on the cash balances (Studwell, 2007).

We have indicated that the duty between a father and son superseded the duty between a man and his sovereign. In Confucian family ethics, a man's duty to his parents even exceeds his duty to his own person. The obedience and deference a man owes his parents does not end on his gaining maturity; he owes his parents unflinching duty as a child, an adolescent, a grown man in his own dotage, and even after his parents' death. This highly personal familial loyalty resounds in two chapters in the *Analects*. Book 4, chapter 19 reads:

> The Master said: While father and mother are still alive, a good son does not wander far afield; or if he does so, goes only where he has said he was going.

Book 19, chapter 18 reads:

> Master Tseng [a pupil of Confucius] said: "I once heard the Master say, filial piety such as that of Meng Chuang Tzu might in other respects be possible to imitate; but the way in which he changed neither his father's servants nor his father's domestic policy, that would indeed be hard to emulate."

The son need not have morally maintained his father's domestic policies and servants because of the concepts of personal loyalty in Chinese culture. The gentleman owed loyalty to the Way and to his prince, not to the state; loyalty to the father constituted loyalty to the father's person and memory, not to the father's friends and subordinates. The reverse also holds true; subordinates owe loyalty to their masters, not to their successors and heirs. Hence, Confucius' amazement stemmed from the son's continuing to maintain his father's servants, and also from the servants' continuing to owe loyalty to the heir. This concept of duty sheds light on the evolution of Chinese business relationships over the centuries, and on understanding some of the human resource practices and succession difficulties in many Chinese business enterprises today. Heirs sometimes do not feel the need to maintain continuity in the family business. Feuding after the patriarch's death can assume vicious proportions, leading to dissolution of the company. For example, Singapore food and beverage maker Yeo Hiap Seng slipped out of the founding Yeo family's control in 1994. This resulted from a bitter family feud in the wake of the death nine years earlier of the patriarch and founder, Yeo Thian In.

MENCIUS

The Second Sage

MENCIUS WAS BORN IN THE state of Lu in 372 BC and died in 289 BC. He served as Confucius' greatest adherent, and without him, our understanding of Confucius' philosophy would prove very different. Mencius did not just follow Confucius; he also contributed to Confucianism, including the prevalent Confucian view on human nature. Thus, he ensured that Confucianism would appear as a humanistic philosophy championing the inherent goodness of mankind. He introduced into Confucianism the concept that morality formed part of human nature, just as did base appetites. In direct opposition to Confucius' view, he argued that if a ruler ceased to govern for the people's benefit, the people had the right to rebel.

In his own life, Confucius influenced only an elite group of educated courtiers. Mencius, more than anyone else, defeated the schools of philosophy that challenged Confucian principles of self-sacrifice, filial piety, and duty. Yang Chu's philosophy of egoism seemed extremely attractive to some elements of society because it freed them of duty to sacrifice for society or their family. Mo Tzu's universal love argument also proved attractive to many. China would have evolved as a less introspective and isolationist country had Mo's philosophy dominated, but it would also have deemphasized duties to family, society, and proper behavior. One must also wonder whether Mo's extreme pacifism could have survived the violence of the many invasions, both physical and spiritual (such as Britain's opium smuggling), that China suffered over the years. Without Mencius, Confucius's name and philosophy might have died a few decades after Confucius did.

Though Confucius would seem to owe Mencius a tremendous debt, Mencius' service and the intertwining of their two names throughout history seems fair. Mencius was born some 100 years after Confucius died, but their relationship began during Confucius' lifetime. Mencius' surname, Mang, and his birthplace in the state of Lu, indicate that his family was one of the three great families usurping power in the state from the Zhou dynasty; their usurpation of power caused the collapse of Confucius' promising early career within the local bureaucracy.

The Relationships and Ethical Behavior

The influential Chinese philosophical systems have historically stressed high ethical standards. Buddhism, a philosophy originating in India, much like Western ethical systems, focuses on the individual's ethical duties and on behavior directly. For example, lying constitutes unethical behavior; ethical dilemmas arise when circumstances conjure a cost to truthfulness, such as hurting loved ones' feelings.

China's Confucianism and Taoism focus their ethical systems on those areas where dilemmas arise in Buddhist and Western ethics, in the area of relationships between people. With its constant focus on individual interaction within society, Confucianism concentrates on five dyadic relationships. In each, the inferior member of the relationship owes a greater duty to the superior member than the other way around. The Five Relationships, from superior person to inferior person, occur from:

1. Sovereign to minister
2. Father to son
3. Husband to wife
4. Older to younger (some maintain it should be older brother–younger brother)
5. Friendship

Taoism, which arose in China either slightly before or concurrently with Confucianism, concentrates on six bidirectional Relations. These relations appear more confining than those in Confucianism because they begin and end within the family. The Six Relations occur between:

1. Father and son
2. Elder brother and younger brother
3. Husband and wife

These Chinese ethical frameworks encapsulate all ethical duties; consequently, what ethical duties does the individual owe people falling outside these frameworks? Two traditional paths handle this dilemma in Confucianism. The first path argues that no true strangers exist. Some Confucians have argued that individuals have the duty to get to know unknown people with whom they interact; hence, they no longer remain strangers but become friends. The second path applies the Taoist formulation of elder brother–younger brother, arguing that all men are brothers, and hence, the relationship between strangers becomes one between elder and younger brothers. Regardless of whether the individual recognizes that all men are brothers or should be friends, the stranger will either be older or younger, and hence, the duties of either elder to younger or younger to elder will follow. Confucians argue that those following the Way will have no enemies, and so no ethical duties accrue to enemies.

Maintenance of social harmony constitutes another ethical duty within Confucianism. Consequently, public displays of disharmony in the family occur rarely, and cause financial speculation and some consternation when they do. For example, when Li Ka-shing's younger son, Richard, engaged in a rebellion by setting up his own company, STAR TV, and taking over Hong Kong Telecom without informing his father, the Chinese media noted that father and son did not fit the harmonious Confucian mores, and gossip columns buzzed. This requirement to maintain social harmony also intrudes on ethical concerns because someone treated unethically will resent this unethical treatment, and the resentment will result in social disharmony through efforts to obtain retribution or justice.

Confucianism entertains very high—but also contextual, and some say situational—ethical standards. Westerners usually view situational ethics as employing flexible ethical standards for opportunistic benefits. Such negative connotations interfere with a true understanding of Confucian ethical standards. Confucian ethical standards, though contextual, are not situational. Confucian ethical standards do vary much more than those within a single Western society or culture, but they actually possess much less flexibility. In Confucian societies, relationships determine the precise ethical behaviors and duties individuals owe each other; variation in duty has little to do with the situation and everything to do with the context imposed by the relationships for which the standards abide. Hence, rather than one ethical standard applying to all people equally, as is found in Western ethical thought, in Confucian societies, as many as seven standards may exist, one for each of the five relationships. For those who cannot accept that all people fall into one of the five relationships but believe in maintaining social harmony, a sixth standard exists. Finally, for those who refuse to accept that all men fall within one of the five relationships and recognize that not all people can adversely affect social harmony, there is a seventh standard. In all instances, the particular situation has minimal effects on the individual's duties.

Little of Yang Chu's writing survives; most of his ethical philosophy comes to us through others' commentaries. Taoist principles greatly influenced Yang Chu's basically Confucian philosophies. One of his Taoist beliefs involved mankind's inherently evil nature. The two traditions disagreed on how to deal with this evil nature: Yang Chu advocated extreme egoism, but Taoism argued for the withdrawal of man from active participation in nature. Thus, scholars have generally represented Taoism as advocating high moral principles. In Taoism, however, outside forces imposed high moral principles on mankind. Mankind could achieve high morality only if it is thrust on them by forces external to their own nature. These forces included their own force of will, fear of punishment, and rationality, among others. One of Lao Tzu's duality paradoxes of Taoism logically implies that if one wishes one's associates to treat one ethically, one should act unethically toward them. This conclusion follows from this verse, in chapter 18 of book 1 of the *Tao Te Ching*:

When the great way falls into disuse
There are benevolence and rectitude;
When cleverness emerges
There is great hypocrisy;
When the six relations are at variance
There are filial children;
When the state is benighted
There are loyal ministers.

Differing Ethical Concepts

The West frowns on, or ignores, many basic principles of business relations among Confucian societies such as the Overseas Chinese; the reverse also holds as the Overseas Chinese frown on or ignore many basic principles of doing business in Western societies. Xiaotong Fei, the father of Chinese sociology, in his 1992 book *From the Soil: The Foundation of Chinese Society,* argued that the differences between Eastern and Western societies went beyond cultural differences to what he called a civilizational chasm; these arguments extend to their business societies. Fei argued that to compare Western and Eastern cultures, one must address both societies' foundations. Western societies draw on transcendental monotheism. Consequently, Western ethical concepts and perceptions of mankind's position in the world begin with mankind's relationship with God; they generally have universal prescriptions such as "Thou shalt not lie." Conversely, in many Eastern societies, such as those of the Overseas Chinese, the Heavens constitute a given not discussed at length. Consequently, Eastern ethical concepts and perceptions of mankind's position in the world draw on the relationships operating at the time; the dominance and direction of the relationships stem from "natural orders": husband over wife, elder over younger, sovereign over minister. In Eastern

LAO TZU

His Own Ultimate Duality Paradox

MANY BELIEVE THAT LAO TZU was an older contemporary of Confucius. The name Lao Tzu actually means "the Old Man." Some believe he was a man named Li, a historian in charge of the Zhou dynasty's archives and often called Tan the Historian. Others declare that he was a man named Lao Lai Tzu, who was born in the same state, Ch'u, as Tan the Historian, and was a contemporary of both Confucius and Tan. Both men's historical biographies record a meeting between Confucius and Lao Tzu in which the latter bested the former. The meeting occurred when Confucius came to Lao Tzu for instruction in the rites. Depending on whether a supporter of Confucius recounts the story, Confucius returns, either showing respect for Lao Tzu's age and great wisdom; or if the story is told by a detractor of Confucius, Confucius admits that Lao Tzu had an understanding far beyond his own.

Traditionally, Lao Tzu retired from public life and was leaving to seek the contemplative life of a holy hermit when the Keeper of the Pass out of the realm of the Zhou Empire to the West asked Lao Tzu to write a book for him. In response to the request, Lao Tzu wrote the *Tao Te Ching,* in which he explains the meaning of the Way and virtuous behavior. Though he wrote it in 5,000 Chinese characters, the *Tao Te Ching* today consists of some 5,250 characters. It has become the most translated book of Chinese literature and philosophy. Lao Tzu then passed through the gates to his life of meditation and into history as one of the world's greatest philosophers. Lore has him living for at least 160 years, and some say for more than 200 years.

Just as he would have intimated in one of his duality paradoxes, however, the harder historians try to establish his existence the more evasive his physical essence becomes, and finally he simply disappears. Chinese historians record his meeting with Confucius taking place in 518 BC; yet they also record his son as a general in the Principality of Wei's army in 273 BC. Also, many stories exist of meetings between Confucius and elder scholars who severely outclassed Confucius. Confucius' critics spread these stories over the years in order to undermine his philosophical credibility.

societies, one's humanity derives from proper role playing in this natural order, not from individuality as in the West.

In the Confucian ethical system that dominates Chinese culture, human relationships, with the foundation of the family, prescribe appropriate behaviors and standards. Behaviors clearly specified within Confucian thought demand rigid conformity to preserve morality; there is little flexibility. The behaviors have to synchronize with clearly specified rites that often cover detailed contexts and include minutiae such as the proper length for a garment sleeve (right and left sleeves had to be of different lengths). On the other hand, virtually any behavior outside contexts covered by Confucian thought that does not cause significant social disharmony proves acceptable and moral. Importantly, because of Chinese relationships' extremely personal nature, personal relationships must exist for there to be ethical duties.

Additionally, Western systems of thought establish different relational norms and practices for nonfamily relationships, and especially for business relationships. In Confucian societies, business relations basically extend family relations. This ethical difference has had a dramatic effect on many aspects of cross-national business. Because all relationships extend familial relationships, behaviors deemed acceptable only within families in Western nations, such as accepting a business partner's word as collateral, can rise to accepted practice in Chinese business relationships.

In recent decades, as Asian markets, economies, and trade become increasingly important, Western multinationals and local Asian businesses have reported a greater number of ethical conflicts and misunderstandings, especially involving the sanctity of signed contracts and intellectual property rights. These misunderstandings may stem from differing ethical concepts. For example, Acer Computers had to establish an office in the U.S. to monitor its own technological activities, and issue warnings when Acer's worldwide operations had appeared about to violate intellectual property rights; Acer's Taiwanese management at its headquarters often failed to realize when they might have inadvertently violated property rights. We will discuss similar misunderstandings, and methods to circumvent them, in the following chapters.

CHAPTER 3

The Overseas Chinese Today: Not the Family Business, But the Family as a Business

> When I was asked by a friend if I would consider managing a family control-
> led corporation, my reaction was, "You must be joking."
>
> —**Koh Boon Hwee,** former executive chairman, Wuthelam Group, when first offered
> the position

Western academics, media, and managers have increased scru-
tiny of Asian business practices as the Asian economies assume
importance for global trade and markets. Yet lack of systematic
information and a paucity of coherent theories of the regional
business cultures often limit their gaining true comprehension
of business practices in the region. Drawing on our research and
experiences with regional companies, and our grasp of the region's
historical and cultural roots, we develop an understanding of the
business environments of the Overseas Chinese networks that dominate Southeast Asian economies and increasingly compete with
multinational corporations from the West, Japan, and Korea. In this,
the third and last of our foundation chapters, we trace the Overseas
Chinese philosophical and cultural roots into their present-day
business environments to paint a fuller picture of the New Asian
Emperors as a people and as a business force.

First, we describe some general characteristics of Chinese networks. Next, we elaborate on the historical and environmental circumstances that shaped the Overseas Chinese networks. In the ensuing section, we describe some cultural characteristics that distinguish the Overseas Chinese from the major Asian competitors, the Japanese. Finally, we examine how informal networks blend into and reinforce the Overseas Chinese companies' formal structures.

What Is a Chinese Network?

Xiaotong Fei (1992) identified five distinctive general characteristics of Chinese networks:

1. They are discontinuous.
2. They have hierarchical and dyadic ties.
3. They emphasize uprightness.
4. They view morality as contextual.
5. They have flexible boundaries that change with circumstances.

Discontinuity

Unlike Westerners, the Chinese do not distinguish among work-related, family-related, and socially related networks, all of which fuse together for them. As we mentioned in Chapter 1, the Overseas Chinese networks have five bases: clan, language, location, guild, and trust. The Overseas Chinese participate in more than one type of network, and membership in one does not guarantee membership in another. For example, one can serve as a member of a clan-based network, a locality-based network, a linguistically based network, and possibly a guild-based network, and each network will usually (though not always) have independence from the others. Additionally, guild-based networks have regional specifications.

Individuals enjoy unique duties, responsibilities, and authorities within a network and across networks, empowering them differently to take action on behalf of their business. In an Overseas Chinese business network or company, individuals with similar titles may exercise drastically differing levels of authority and responsibility, and their stature may vary across networks, affecting their overall power.

Consequently, Overseas Chinese businessmen seeking partners can choose from several networks—though they must do so with care. An ally within one network may oppose projects or business partners in another as interests clash. Generally, though, Chinese businessmen avoid generating opposition and work on creating support.

Hierarchical and dyadic ties

Relationships within networks approximate dyadic and directional relations within Confucian families (described in the previous chapter); the relationships' superior members define the relationships. Individuals have direct relationships with all the networks' members. Those with higher stature within a dyad have the upper hand within the relationship. Respect within networks is often derived from one's ability to move flawlessly from a dominant role to a subordinate role and back to dominant within the network, depending on one's position relative to the people one interacts with in business and social activities. The required duties, responsibilities, and behaviors can vary significantly according to relative positions within networks. Individuals' relative positions can also vary with recent performance, especially among younger members trying to establish themselves. Thus, keeping track of everyone's relative position, especially in a large network, may prove monumental. Unlike younger members, older members generally enjoy more stability because they automatically retain rank and prestige through age and seniority.

THE FEDERATION OF HOKKIEN ASSOCIATIONS OF MALAYSIA

A Traditional Dialect Network

THE FEDERATION OF HOKKIEN Associations of Malaysia forms Malaysia's preeminent dialect federation. It serves as the peak body of Hokkien associations in Malaysia. Some of the country's most prominent business-men serve or have served on its executive committee, including the late Lim Goh Tong, head of the Genting Group; Tiong Hiew King, controller of the Rimbunan Hijau timber and logging company; and the late Loh Boon Siew, controller of the Boon Siew Group. The federation has 138 affiliated associations. Most of the members have relatively traditional outlooks and tend to have a Chinese education. Despite its Hokkien membership, the federation conducts business in Mandarin because many Hokkien subdialects are mutually unintelligible.

The federation, active in business, formed Hoklian Holdings, its business arm, almost two decades ago. Apart from its Malaysian investments, the company signed an agreement with the Anxi subprovince in Fujian, China, to build a hotel and is also engaging in other investments there. Anxi is the ancestral region for several senior federation executives. The federation receives regular visits from Anxi business delegations.

The federation actively conducts international meetings and exchanges with other Hokkien associations worldwide.

In doing business with the Overseas Chinese, foreign managers should garner as much information as possible on the individuals they deal with regularly or occasionally, or plan to deal with in the future. Relative positions of both the Overseas Chinese and the foreign managers mold expectations. Also, foreign managers should remember that older members of Chinese business organizations often enjoy significantly greater power and influence than their official title may indicate.

Uprightness

Uprightness involves the ability and willingness to behave as expected at the appropriate time and in the appropriate fashion. In the West, trust arises when people gain a reputation for doing what they say they will do. In the Chinese sense, trust has two elements. The first involves the same concept of trust as the West employs; the second involves uprightness. Uprightness constitutes an important behavioral ideal, and without it, complete trust in the Chinese sense cannot exist.

Western managers failing to perform as expected encounter problems in dealing with Overseas Chinese businessmen. The Overseas Chinese will perceive the Westerner as not upright and withdraw accordingly. Conversely, the Western managers, who may have acted in good faith, will see their business relationships disintegrate and usually press harder for closure. In many Southeast and East Asian countries dominated by the Overseas Chinese, Western managers may initially invest in good guides for help with the formalities. A good guide may aid in preserving upright behavior until the Western managers have gained experience and established a local reputation. Because of the emphasis on personal relationships, the Western managers' local reputations will establish the degree of trust and loyalty extended to their company by the networks—even for companies active in Asia for decades.

THE CYBER BUSINESS NETWORK

I N 1995, THE SINGAPORE CHINESE Chamber of Commerce and Industry (SCCCI) formally launched on the Internet what it labeled a new tribal network: the World Chinese Business Network (WCBN). With connections to Chinese chambers of commerce worldwide, the WCBN provided a global computer network to link ethnic Chinese executives and a massive database containing information on businesses run by the Overseas Chinese. According to the SCCCI, "The WCBN is aimed at strengthening the networking of Chinese businessmen throughout the world. It is designed to help Chinese businessmen worldwide in establishing contacts and exchanging information with one another in a speedy and systematic manner." The Singaporean Minister for Information and the Arts, Brigadier General George Yeo, emphasized that tribal networks will become very important in the future and "a lot of business will be done over these networks."

The WCBN, a brainchild of Senior Minister Lee Kuan Yew, constituted the first online global link for Chinese traders. In 1993, at the Second World Chinese Entrepreneurs Convention, Senior Minister Lee proposed that the networking of the Overseas Chinese be made efficient by providing relevant data on the Internet. With the technical assistance of the Institute of Systems Science and Netcenter (Singapore) and a financial grant of US$100,000 from Singapore's National Science and Technology Board, the SCCCI then proceeded to undertake the US$500,000 project. The WCBN furnished detailed corporate information on more than 15,000 Overseas Chinese companies from some 15 countries on subsidiaries, products, marketing, and distribution operations. One can access information in both English and Chinese through typing in key words. However, Yeo quickly observed that such business networks could only amount to "public domains" for the transfer of information; companies would have to move into the "private domain" to strike deals. "In the corporate world, those who can make more money are those who have more information than others. We all know that while some information can be made freely available, some must be kept confidential," BG Yeo said.

In 1999, the WCBN was renamed the Cyber Business Network (CBN) and its mission was redefined. The CBN now has the mission of making technology more accessible to its clients and generating efficient and cost-effective processes for automation, procurement, and sourcing. Though it no longer seeks to serve as an exclusively tribal network for the Overseas Chinese, the strongest markets remain in Asia, with the bulk of the clients and partners being of Southeast Asian origin, and offices in its Singapore home, Hong Kong, and soon in China.

The CBN may be accessed on the Internet at http://www cbn.com.sg; the service is currently free of charge.

Contextual morality

As we discussed in detail in Chapter 2, among the Overseas Chinese, ethical standards vary with the business relationship. Longer and better-established relationships with equals or superiors entail higher standards than shorter, fleeting relationships with inferiors.

Western companies should also remember the personal nature of relationships among the Overseas Chinese. Many Western companies rotate executives through Asian subsidiaries and offices. However, their incoming executives do not automatically inherit the outgoing executives' goodwill and strong relationships (or even their opponents). Traditionally, companies have not owned franchises of trust and uprightness in Asia; individuals have. From the increased familiarity that Chinese and Asian business people are acquiring with Western companies, this is changing with respect to established, well-known companies.

Flexible boundaries

Among the Overseas Chinese, the boundaries of a network have flexibility and vary with circumstances much more so than among Western networks. Chinese networks exhibit very personal, though relatively low-strength, ties of loyalty. Individuals' personal networks expand and contract with their relative success (as personal contacts do for Westerners); individuals' networks for business projects vary with partners, locality, and the nature of the project. A plethora of circumstantial factors (too many to enumerate) may affect the precise make-up of an individual's business network in any one instance.

Consequently, Western managers find it difficult to judge whom to contact, or how much to divulge to potential partners. Also, the wrong choice of partners (for example, one viewed as untrustworthy or not upright) can cause difficulties for a company for an extended period of time.

We now discuss some historical and environmental effects on the evolution of the Overseas Chinese networks.

Historical and Environmental Effects on the Overseas Chinese Business Networks

Many Overseas Chinese, especially those in Hong Kong and Taiwan, started as merchants and traders. Trading was the predominant business for the merchant-class families in China. These Overseas

Chinese left China as factors and representatives for prosperous traders, usually blood relations from their home district. Other
Overseas Chinese, especially those in Southeast Asia, left China
as coolies to work for Chinese and European traders, planta-
tion owners, and government and semigovernmental authorities.
They worked hard, lived extremely frugally, and saved money until they
could strike out on their own (Chan and Chiang, 1994). Once these
Overseas Chinese gained some degree of prosperity, they often
moved into property-related businesses, and then into any business
deemed profitable.

Table 3.1 presents a small sample of Overseas Chinese families and the businesses in which they operate. The founders of the
Overseas Chinese companies, though highly intelligent, generally had little formal education and even less formal Western-style
business education. Generally, these patriarchs resembled generations of Western businessmen before the founding of the great
(and not-so-great) Western business schools. However, significant
factors distinguished the Overseas Chinese patriarchs' upbringing and training and differentiated them from their Western
counterparts.

The business education of the founders of today's major
Overseas Chinese companies originated from their experience and
training in Confucian village schools. The expansion of their business followed the dictates of their education, culture, and experience. Their education and culture showed the Confucian emphasis
on the family and employed the Confucian perspective of societal relationships as extensions of, yet subordinate to, familial
relationships.

The experiences of the Overseas Chinese companies' patriarchs
in China and their new homelands reinforced their Confucian
perspective of relying only on family or a select network. Back in
China, the philosophers traditionally considered merchants as the
lowest class of humanity; the government persecuted merchants for

TABLE 3.1: *Some Families and Businesses of the Overseas Chinese Business Networks*

Family/Leader	Forbes Rank*	Primary Businesses
Indonesia		
Liem Sioe Liong and Anthony Salim	N/A	Cement, processed foods, flour milling, steel, leisure, real estate, and investments
Eka Tjipta Widjaja	N/A	Pulp and paper, agribusiness, financial services, palm oil, and property
Mochtar Riady	N/A	Property, retailing, and health care
Suhargo Gondokusumo	N/A	Agri-industries and property
Prajogo Pangestu	N/A	Timber and car assembly
Sukanto Tanoto	284	Paper, pulp, palm oil, and real estate
Malaysia		
Robert Kuok	97	See Kuok family under Hong Kong
Quek Leng Chan	524	Finance and diversified investments
Lim Kok Thay	N/A	Casinos and real estate
Vincent Tan	N/A	Leisure, manufacturing, investment, and cable TV
Philippines		
Lucio Tan	785	Beer, tobacco, banking, education, and investment
Henry Sy	843	Retailing, banking, cement, and investment
Alfonso Yuchengco	N/A	Banking and insurance
Antonio Cojuangco	N/A	Telecommunications and real estate
John Gokongwei	N/A	Real estate, petrochemicals, financial services, power, and aviation
Thailand		
Chearavanont family	897	Agribusiness, real estate, retailing, and telecommunications
Kanjanapas family	N/A	Real estate, transport, and finance
Ratanarak family	N/A	Cement, banking, and telecommunications
Sophonpanich family	N/A	Banking, real estate, and investments
Lamsam family	N/A	Banking and real estate

TABLE 3.1 (*Continued*)

Family/Leader	Forbes Rank*	Primary Businesses
Hong Kong		
Kuok family	23	Real estate, banking, hotels, and infrastructural development
Lee Shau-Kee	29	Real estate, fuel, transportation, hotels, and resorts
Li Ka-shing	11	Real estate, construction, infrastructural developments, and utilities
Pao family	N/A	Real estate, cable television, infrastructural developments, and transportation
Singapore		
Kwek Leng Beng	N/A	Real estate, hotels, and financial services
Ng Teng Fong	132	Real estate, hotels, food, and beverages
Khoo family	N/A	Hotels and real estate
Wee Cho Yaw	396	Banking, real estate, and hotels
Lee Seng Wee	N/A	Banking, plantations, insurance, and trading
Goh Cheng Liang	N/A	Paint and manufacturing
Oei Hong Leong	N/A	Investments and diversified businesses
Macao		
Stanley Ho	113	Real estate and casinos
Taiwan		
Stan Shih	N/A	Information technology and communications
Tsai family	120	Insurance, real estate, and construction
Wang family	178	Petrochemicals, plastics, and diversified manufacturing
Wu Tung Chin	N/A	Real estate, insurance, banking, retailing, and diversified manufacturing
Hsu Yu Ziang	707	Textiles, retailing, cement, and conglomerate diversification
Koo family	N/A	Banking, cement, and diversified financial services

* *Rank among Forbes 2008 list of billionaires. N/A does not necessarily mean that a family is not worthy of a ranking on the billionaires list but often means that no one family member can be identified as having sufficient wealth to make the list. For example, in its list of the wealthiest Singaporeans, Forbes cites the Khoo family as Singapore's second wealthiest family but does not rank the family in its billionaires list.*

their mobility, and especially so when that mobility involved contact with foreigners. In their new overseas homes, the local governments and people often admired the business skills of the Overseas Chinese; but as communities of outsiders without the protection of their home country government, the Overseas Chinese were convenient scapegoats for colonial and local governments to blame for policy mistakes and disasters. In Batavia, 10,000 Overseas Chinese were massacred. In the Spanish colony of the Philippines, non-Catholic Chinese were periodically persecuted, and occasionally massacred; in one such event, about 25,000 Chinese were massacred in the Manila-based Chinese community alone. British colonial governors also frequently encouraged feuds between the Overseas Chinese secret societies; these governors provoked local internal conflict and withheld peacekeeping troops until they felt a sufficient number of Overseas Chinese had been killed (Wang, 1991; Fernandez-Armesto, 1995).

THE INDONESIAN FAMILY CONGLOMERATES

One for All and All for One

THE OVERSEAS CHINESE BUSINESS groups control more than 33 major interlinked conglomerates in Indonesia. In recent years, interlinkages occurred through cross-shareholdings and directorships, joint ventures, and family links such as marriages between the major business families. Overseas Chinese business groups linked by family connections include the Lippo Group and the Myapada Group; the Lippo Group and Panin Bank; the Gadjah Tunggal Group and the Ometraco Group; the Gunung Sewu Group and the Dharmala Group; and the Gemala Group and the Danamon Group. Many of these Overseas Chinese business groups rose to prominence during the three-decade-long rule (1967–1998) of General Suharto.

The interlinkages turned potential competitors into colleagues, allowing the business groups to access new sources of capital and maintain market share. Management of political risk is an important by-product of the interlinkages. If the Indonesian government, in the form of one of President Suharto's successors such as the present office holder, President Susilo Bambang Yudhoyono, turns unfavorable toward even one business group, the interlinkages ensure that the unfavorable currents will flow onto most of the others and ensure their survival. Consequently, each business group has a vested interest in maintaining all the others' interests. A good example of this occurred after the financial crisis when the Salim Group, once the largest Overseas Chinese business group in Indonesia and closely linked to General Suharto, became a target of the general's opponents, and a symbolic target of those tired of his regime's corruption. Salim lost control of some of its businesses; however, under Anthony Salim, the present family patriarch and group founder Liem Sioe Liong's successor, the group has clawed its way back into the top echelon of Indonesia's business world. Political leaders in Indonesia have challenged individual conglomerates and campaigned against the old ways of doing business. Yet they have not challenged the business groups' economic position as a whole

for fear of widespread economic repercussions. The Overseas
Chinese business groups have absorbed political uncertainty in
Indonesia by arraying themselves as interdependent dominos.

Some Overseas Chinese businesses had links to key members of the Suharto family through joint ventures. After the
Asian financial crisis, the businesses built relationships with
his successor's well-connected associates. These *pribumi,* or
ethnic Indonesian politicians, generally bring small amounts
of equity to the joint ventures and achieve a high proportion
of the profits. Yet the *pribumis* also often bring political capital, negotiating bureaucratic and regulatory obstacles for their
business associates, and thereby earning high returns on their
political capital.

These circumstances created a people fiercely loyal to their families and network partners and dependent on one another rather than
any governing authorities. The Overseas Chinese also displayed a
pronounced preference for maintaining a significant proportion of
their wealth in liquid forms and for physically dispersed rather than
concentrated fixed investments. Liquid assets proved convenient in
forced flight, and physically dispersed investments provided geographical diversity, hedging risks in anti-Chinese attacks.

Physically dispersed fixed assets also reinforced the networks
among family businesses. The Overseas Chinese trusted only close
associates; local onsite managers had to have extensive independent authority to disburse assets quickly given slow communica-
tion systems and perilous times. The increasingly diversified assets
and growing physical dispersion hindered constant surveillance
and guidance from the head of the family business. Consequently,
purely trust-based relations emerged as a potent force in the
networks.

Despite their great fortunes, most of the new Asian Emperors maintained relatively small individual companies that could be considered large only collectively. The small companies precluded the confiscation or destruction of any one company from seriously affecting an overall financial position. Second, without primogeniture and with the normal emphasis on large families that most traditional cultures have, the Overseas Chinese envisioned their companies dissolving after the death of the patriarch. Dissecting a larger company would create greater economic dislocation for the family than distributing a bunch of smaller, unrelated companies. Consequently, Overseas Chinese companies rarely achieved economies of scale or scope to become effective international competitors; those that did achieve large size often came crashing down after the founder's death. The best of the New Asian Emperors, such as Li Ka-shing of Hong Kong, have smaller families, and their children (almost always their sons) inherit the greater part of the estate.

The Confucian emphasis on personal relationships, with the historical lack of institutional support from government agencies, reinforced the Overseas Chinese emphasis on personal relationships. These combined factors also ensured that families and their businesses never separated. Though many Overseas Chinese companies form legal corporations, and the family bases of some companies appear weak, most families still control their companies either outright or through network partners with whom the families share projects and interlocking directorates.

As Table 3.1 shows, the Overseas Chinese have generally not focused on primary businesses, often displaying extreme conglomerate diversification. Other business networks in developing countries, such as the Overseas Indian networks and Latin American *grupos,* also display unrelated conglomerate diversification (Haley and Haley, 1998, 1999). In the last century, as the United States industrialized, many American companies engaged in unrelated diversification (Heilbroner and Singer, 1984). Yet the Overseas

Chinese appear to have taken unrelated conglomerate diversification to a new level. With New Asian Emperor Robert Kuok, one is hard pressed to find a business in which he does not engage: food, luxury and middle-market hotels, real estate, sugar and oil palm plantations, newspapers (including the world's most profitable newspaper, the *South China Morning Post*). He has large investments in Indonesia, Hong Kong, China, Australia, Malaysia, Singapore, the Philippines, and Thailand. He owns a piece of CITIC Pacific, the Beijing-controlled conglomerate, and the Beijing World Trade Center. His acumen is the only glue for his diverse business interests; as Kuok describes his role, "I am the little string that ties the rings together" (Tanzer, 1997).

ROBERT KUOK

Network Zen Master

IF ANYONE WERE PROCLAIMED A ZEN master of networking, it would be Malaysian-born, Singapore-educated Robert Kuok. His skill at managing within the network's structure has earned him the sobriquet of the "world's shrewdest businessman" from *Forbes* magazine. Just like many other prominent Overseas Chinese businessmen, Kuok has substantial operations in several countries. Pinpointing·some of his companies' headquarters can often prove confusing. Sometimes a company's operations become so closely associated with a host country that each subsidiary appears local. The Far East

Group, headed by tycoon Ng Teng Fong, is such an example. Far East Group has substantial stakes in both Hong Kong and Singapore, and in both instances (Far East in Singapore and Sinoland in Hong Kong) the operations seem local.

With other companies, situations may arise similar to the Kuok Group's and company headquarters may become mobile. Singapore served as Kuok's first headquarters because of the company's early emphasis on trading and Singapore's position as an entrepôt. Singapore's position as headquarters was further enhanced after he founded his phenomenally successful Shangri-La Hotel chain with its flagship hotel in Singapore. Later, according to rumors, Kuok moved his headquarters to Malaysia because of differences with the local authorities, and many still consider him a Malaysian businessman. He has vast holdings in properties, plantations, utilities, and dozens of other businesses in Malaysia. In the 1970s, he earned the title of the Sugar King because he controlled 10 percent of the world's sugar trade. Regardless, Hong Kong hosts his headquarters these days; members of his family steer various businesses in different countries. Though Hong Kong plays official host to the Kuok Group's headquarters, operationally the other nodes in Kuok's network web can equal the headquarters in importance, and sometimes surpass it.

Seemingly proving the Confucian argument for bias against merchants, Kuok has demonstrated extreme mobility, moving headquarters from one location and state to another. Sometimes he moves for convenience, sometimes for political reasons, and sometimes for strategic preferences. Mostly, the Network Zen Master doesn't care to explain his reasons.

The Overseas Chinese are generally an independent lot. Faced with harsh economic realities and experiences that contradicted their cultural teachings, they rebelled. Their culture advised marginal acceptability of the profit motive; their governments advocated accepting their inferior lot in life. Yet they rejected cultural arguments and government restrictions and fought for their families' livelihood. In a culture emphasizing conformity, they refused to conform. This refusal to conform, of course, constituted a uniquely Confucian rebellion—that of a group's refusal to conform rather than any individual's. The groups within their membership required the same degree of conservative conformity as the societies against which they were rebelling; the groups rebelled because the dominant groups, or networks, or members did.

We have discussed some powerful influences on the Overseas Chinese; but throughout their history, these hardy people have encountered diverse influences that have honed their intellectual agility and enhanced their adaptability. Most of the New Asian Emperors have faced human nature and confronted harsh economic realities; most have lived under colonial and noncolonial governments with legal systems completely foreign to the Confucian mind. In Southeast Asia, Thailand alone eluded colonial rule. Hong Kong reverted to Chinese control in 1997; Macao, Portugal's colony next to Hong Kong, reverted to Chinese control in 1999. Consequently, Robert Kuok could say, "I adapt like a chameleon to the particular society where I am operating at the moment." Robert Riley, managing director of Mandarin Oriental Hotel Group and a fierce competitor of Kuok's, said, "He's a local everywhere he goes" (Tanzer, 1997).

Western managers should remember that the Overseas Chinese managers, unlike their counterparts in Korea and Japan, have tremendous capability for radical action. Because of most companies' authoritarian nature, individuals with sufficient stature can make and implement decisions blazingly fast. We now compare the Overseas Chinese business culture with that of the Japanese.

Distinguishing Cultural Traits

Several authors have argued that Asia will follow Japan's techno-logical trajectory in a flying-geese formation (Yamashita, 1991). Nakamura (1992) extended the flying-geese, Japan-dominated per-spective of Asian development to strategic management by argu-ing that strategic decision making in Asia was evolving as it did in Japan; the developing Asian countries were following Japan as flying geese follow a leader. Although certain similarities exist between the Japanese economy's evolution and that of the other Asian nations, significant economic and cultural differences indicate flaws in Nakamura's arguments. This section elaborates on the region-specific characteristics that differentiate the Overseas Chinese cul-ture from that of their Japanese competitors.

Like the Japanese, most Asian economies are managed econo-mics that have depended primarily on export-led growth; however, key differences lie in the sources and directions of their exports. Japanese companies have always formed the country's principal source of exports, and until recently, Japanese exports focused on North America and Europe. Among those economies dominated by the Overseas Chinese, manufacturing-based multinational corpo-rations have been the principal source of exports to Western nations; the Overseas Chinese and other local companies have primarily con-centrated on the local markets that Western companies now per-ceive as so important (Haley and Tan, 1996; Haley and Haley, 1998, 1999). As we establish in the next chapter, local Asian markets con-stitute an informational void for market-related information on which so many corporate decisions depend in the West (Haley and Tan, 1996). Overseas Chinese companies have grown and developed their management decision making and management systems primarily in competition with one another in this information-scarce environ-ment, rather than in competition with Western multinational corpo-rations and Western domestic companies in economically mature, information-rich environments. Consequently, the economic similarities between Japan and its Asian neighbors assume less significance.

Table 3.2 (Haley and Haley, 1998, 1999) summarizes some significant cultural differences between the Chinese and Japanese. These cultural differences have influenced the Overseas Chinese network companies, their concepts of loyalty, and the bases for commercial trust and decision making in business dealings—just as the Japanese culture and competitive environments have affected Japanese companies on these issues.

Firm-related attributes

Merchants

The Japanese and Chinese cultures have exhibited opposing attitudes toward merchants. The Japanese culture incorporates an economic

TABLE 3.2: *Cultural Similarities and Differences Between the Chinese and Japanese*

Attributes	Chinese	Japanese
Firm		
Merchants	Reviled	Exalted
Primogeniture	None	Strong
Company's life span	Short	Long
Loyalty		
Family definition	Blood	Role
Focus	Individual	Institution
Intensity	Low	High
Filial piety vs. patriotism	Opposed	Equivalent
Commercial trust		
Ethical foundation	Five Relationships and social harmony	Mutual self-interest
Ethical focus	The Way	Service to father figure
Expectation of benefits	Immediate and up-front	Long-term and delayed

philosophy of growth that exalts merchants. The Confucian culture of the Overseas Chinese, however, exalts peasants and reviles and persecutes merchants. As noted in the previous chapter, Confucian philosophers frowned on merchants, whom they perceived as excessively concerned with profit rather than the Way (Lau, 1995; Legge, 1970; Waley, 1996); the philosophers also saw merchants as mobile, and thus unreliable supporters of rulers. Not surprisingly, innumerable waves of Overseas Chinese flooded South and Southeast Asia over the centuries; every wave corresponded to a period of persecution against merchants.

Primogeniture and company life span

Another difference between Chinese and Japanese customs revolves around primogeniture. These customs have influenced company life span. Confucian customs emphasized large families, banned primogeniture and children shared the inheritance roughly equally—consequently, the ancient Chinese saying, "No fortune survives the third generation." In recent years, the best Overseas Chinese business families have chosen a primary heir, but not necessarily thier eldest son. Thus, Malaysian casino magnate Lim Goh Tong chose Lim Kok Thay over his elder brother; Indonesia's Liem Sioe Liong sidestepped his eldest son, Albert, when he designated Anthony Salim as heir; and Henry Fok circumvented his eldest son, Timothy, in favor of his sibling Ian. Most of today's major Overseas Chinese companies have survived only as far as the second generation of managers (Chu and MacMurray, 1993). Japanese customs, on the other hand, have always emphasized primogeniture, although according to custom, the oldest son need not necessarily inherit. Consequently, wealthy Japanese families have also often bequeathed the family fortune to the most capable sons to build concentrated and continued wealth. Unlike those of the Overseas Chinese, Japanese companies such as Mitsubishi have survived for a considerable time in some form. Indeed, some of Japan's major companies began centuries ago as family companies that evolved through growth, and the military establishment's encouragement in the late 1900s and early 2000s, into the Japanese *keiretsu* conglomerates of today.

Loyalty-related attributes

Family, focus, and intensity

In the Japanese culture, loyalty, though very strong, has a functional base; family members owe filial loyalty to the breadwinner, not to the actual father. Conversely, in the Chinese culture family members owe filial loyalty to the father, regardless of who actually serves as the breadwinner in the family; members of the Overseas Chinese networks share highly personalized, as opposed to functional, bases for loyalty. In the Chinese culture, loyalty accrues to individuals; members often do not transfer loyalty to friends or employers, and hence, employee loyalty frequently does not survive an individual manager or transfer to another company.

Patriotism

The relationships that the Japanese and Chinese perceive between individuals and societies also differ. These associations affect how the Overseas Chinese contribute to their adopted and native countries. A Japanese adage posits that "to be a good patriot is to be a good son." Alternatively, the equivalent adage in China argues that "one cannot be both a good patriot and a good son." Hence, Japanese employees demonstrate intense loyalty to their father figure, their employer, who by extension serves as the emperor's symbolic representative. Conversely, Overseas Chinese employees demonstrate relatively weak loyalty to an employer, unless they work for the family company or have been incorporated into the extended business family.

Trust-related attributes

Ethical foundations

Concepts of ethics differ significantly between the two cultures (Haley, 1997b; Haley and Haley, 1997, 1998, 1999) affecting the bases of commercial trust. In the Japanese view, contractual duties bind and familial and friendship ties help, but ties of personal and corporate mutual self-interest prove paramount; trust in commercial relationships derives from perceived mutual self-interest, hence the numerous social gatherings in which potential business associates seek out similarities in outlooks, perspectives, and values.

As elaborated in the previous chapter, among the Overseas Chinese five relationships define ethical duty: (1) sovereign and minister, (2) father and son, (3) husband and wife, (4) elder brother and younger brother, and (5) friends. If relationships fall outside these categories, then the primary ethical duty involves maintaining social harmony. Specific, contextual relationship-based, normative ethical duties and expected behaviors regulate relationships, not universal constants. Thus, without familial or established friendship ties trust rarely exists in commercial relationships with the Overseas Chinese. To work well with them, foreign business associates must build noncommercial ties of friendship or family. Outside of established relationships, the Overseas Chinese, unconstrained by Western ethical concepts of the level playing field, prove brutal competitors. Confucian societies accept steeply hierarchical structures and inherent inequality of men's aptitudes and stations in life as a necessary condition for social good. Hence, historically, Indonesian Chinese bankers could ethically forward strangers' loan applications as strategically important information to members of their business network doing business in the same area and industry as the loan applicant. Strangers, in some interpretations of Confucian ethics, do not fall within the Confucian contextual framework of ethics and often cannot disrupt social harmony in their disappointment and anger.

Ethical focus

The two cultures' ethics demonstrate different normative focal points. The Overseas Chinese, influenced by Confucian philosophy, believe individuals should behave appropriately to their station within the dyadic framework of their relationships and in accordance with the Way, an established norm of behavior owed to individuals with whom one has a relationship and based on the relative position held in that relationship. Chinese employers may often seem like emperors because businesses serve as an extension of the family and fathers enjoy a preeminent position. To the Japanese, individuals should serve their superiors (their father figures), and through their superiors, patriotically, their emperors. Their loyalty to the company originates from the employer symbolically representing the emperor, rather than from the company representing an extension of the family.

Expectation of benefits

The Overseas Chinese differ from the Japanese in their expectation of benefits from contractual relationships. The Overseas Chinese will enter or maintain contractual relationships only if they receive at least minimal benefits and have the expectation of making greater profits within a relatively short period of time. When the benefits and expectations fade, so do contractual duties for the most part. The Overseas Chinese will invest time, money, and effort, but they expect to see tangible benefits up front (Redding, 1996). The Overseas Chinese, whose history includes many episodes of persecution in Southeast Asia, exhibit a hard-edged negotiating style and expect benefits that match the effort they invest in a project (Redding, 1996). A signed contract may often begin, rather than end, negotiations (Haley and Tan, 1996); consequently, commercial partners should expect some quibbling over the terms. Because of their experience with foreign populations, the Overseas Chinese, unlike the Japanese, desire tangible returns and often maintain substantial holdings of liquid assets (Haley, 1997a). The Japanese have long been known for their willingness to forgo profit in order to build market share.

This section has demonstrated the significant cultural differences that exist between the Chinese and Japanese cultures relating to their business practices. These differences strongly suggest that despite Nakamura's claim (1992), the strategic management practices of the Overseas Chinese differ significantly from those of Japanese firms and are likely to continue to do so. The next section focuses on formal structure and networks in Overseas Chinese companies.

How Networks Permeate Formal Structures

Similar to corporate interlocking in the West, Chinese business networks emerged to reduce and control market uncertainties. The previous sections have outlined how the Overseas Chinese initially lacked assistance from government and simultaneously faced anti-Chinese movements in Southeast Asian countries. Fierce competition for resources and market share in the region also led to intercompany distrust. Networks of interdependent relationships reduced some of the risks for Overseas Chinese businesses, and the business groups nurtured formal structures they could control, using people they could trust in key positions and relying on networks of trust or obligation to do business (Fukuyama, 1995; Redding, 1993; Redding and Hsiao, 1993; Whitley, 1992).

Because of these historical antecedents, ethnic Chinese businesses mirror traditional family structures (see Tsui-Auch, 2006). The families' patriarchs almost always serve as the head of the business. The patriarchs often exercise unquestioned power, and at first, run their business with an inner circle of family members and friends. Over time, the business often decentralizes by assigning sons to branches or business lines (Hamilton, 1997). Complex formal and informal relationships emerge, including cross-holdings and interlocking directorates as well as intragroup trade and transfers of capital, technology, and personnel (Loh, Goh, and Tan, 2000). To maintain control and avoid disclosing company financial information, family members often cannot sell their shares to outsiders. If they need outside equity, the founding family seeks to control a publicly listed company through associated banks and financial or holding companies (Fukuyama, 1995). Generally, Overseas Chinese family businesses offer a minority stake in their public company for outside equity. The family maintains control of its public company through direct investment in equity by other family companies, direct investment in equity by individual family members, cross-holdings with related companies associated with the family groups, cross-directorships with related companies, and transactions that generate control with related parties (Zang, 1999). The Overseas Chinese skillfully forge pyramidal formal structures to handle the contradictory needs of growth and control (Claessens, Djankov, and Lang, 2000). Pyramids are multilevel ownership networks constructed by chains of interorganizational shareholdings, including control structures at the top, a smattering of intermediary companies in the middle, and myriad subordinate companies at the bottom.

The Formosa Plastics Group (FPG), one of Taiwan's largest and most profitable business groups, employs a pyramidal formal structure. The founder, Y. C. Wang, whose achievements won him the title "god of management," passed away on October 18, 2008, in New Jersey. He had flown to the U.S. despite his doctors' opposition to inspect the group's U.S. subsidiaries and to ensure their normal operation amid the prevailing financial storm. Wang was born in Xindian township, Taipei County, in 1917. In 1954, with only an elementary school education, he began his business career by opening a rice store with NT$200 borrowed from his father. Subsequently, he built a business empire that spanned plastics, medical care, biotech, thermal power, and electronics. In 2007, the group's total revenue exceeded NT$1.97 trillion, the second highest in Taiwan, trailing only Hon Hai's NT$2 trillion. In 2007, FPG was also the most profitable group, raking in NT$219.1 billion in after-tax net profits. In 2008, Wang's eldest son, Winston, ran a petrochemical group in China, which he founded after departing FPG over a dispute with his father concerning an extramarital affair. The younger son, Wen-hsiang, headed an FPG subsidiary in the U.S. while two of his daughters, Jui-hua and Jui-yu, held memberships in the Group Administration Office. Wang's family owned controlling shares in three major companies: Formosa Plastic Corporation, Nan Ya Plastic Corporation, and Formosa Chemical and Fiber Corporation. Through these companies, he indirectly controlled the rest of the group (Chung and Mahmood, 2006). Each of these three flagships controlled 33.3 percent of the shares in Formosa Heavy Industry, Tai Su Formosa Plastic Transportation Corporation, and Formosa Fairway Corporation. A similar pattern emerged in Formosa Petrochemical Corporation. Though Wang and his family held only 17.8 and 12.5 percent respectively of the shares in the three major companies, they enhanced their controlling power through mutual shareholdings. Consequently, the family directed the whole business group by maintaining sufficient equity in the controlling center. The pyramidal formal structure also allowed the family to own significant voting rights with minimal cash, and to separate ownership and control.

In summary, networks serve as a buffer for the Overseas Chinese business groups and derive from trust and reliability. Family control and reputation are the main ingredients in constructing a business network. As the next chapter elaborates, unlike Western executives Overseas Chinese companies' owners can make and implement speedy business decisions, which allows them to develop a reputation of reliability and trustworthiness in Chinese business communities. Family control also generates mutual trust among interrelated companies that conduct business on this basis. Company reputation in the broader business environment derives mainly from reliability and key external stakeholders' evaluation of the company's position in commercial hierarchies. In our next chapter, we discuss the strategic-planning environment that exists in Southeast Asia. We speculate on why it exists and discuss the unique strategic planning and decision-making system the Overseas Chinese have developed to take advantage of their special environment, the informational void.

PART II

The Foundations of Analysis

CHAPTER 4

Introduction to an Informational Void: The Black Hole of Southeast Asia

In Chinese business circles, the emphasis is on harmony. People agree to compete or not to compete.

—**Cheung Kim Hung,** *editor-in-chief, Next magazine, Hong Kong*

An old adage posits that the quality of one's decisions depends on the quality of one's information. The more complex the situation, the more important it is that managers have appropriate data to analyze. The information generated through those analyses yields the understanding of the situation necessary to make an optimal decision. Yet managers conducting strategic planning in the prescribed manner in Southeast Asia's complex environments will never have sufficient data to justify taking action. Southeast Asia has always been, and continues to be, an informational black hole (*Economist*, 2001; Haley and Tan, 1996, 1998; Haley and Haley, 1999; Young, 2002). This situation exists regardless of the increasingly important role that Southeast Asia is playing in the world economy.

Many continue to think that the financial crisis of 1997 devastated Southeast Asia; yet the region has risen from the ashes as an economic powerhouse. Without the long shadows of the twin neighboring emerging-market titans of China and India, Southeast

Asia would have regained the mantle of dominant emerging region in the international media. Although foreign capital inflows never returned to pre-crisis levels, the region's high savings rate never faltered. This savings rate allowed domestic capital to lead the reemergence of Southeast Asia; in 2004, Indonesia became the last Southeast Asian country to surpass its pre-crisis per capita income level (*Economist*, 2007).

Despite the economic shocks of 1997, Southeast Asia constitutes a very special market. Over a 40-year period, no economic region in history has grown faster. Unlike Japan and South Korea, which also used export-led growth to spur economic development, Southeast Asia has remained among the freest of markets in the world. Consequently, though Southeast Asian exports have grown significantly over the years, so have its imports. These imports surged when the regional economies embarked on restructuring and value-added manufacturing. Indeed, from 1993 to 1998, Southeast Asia was the only economic region outside North America that served as a net importer of goods. The region's growth fostered jobs and economic growth for other regions of the world. The resulting large trade deficit partially caused the crisis of 1997. In 2007, the countries hit by the 1997 crisis were maintaining trade surpluses. While outlier Malaysia's trade surplus approximated 11 percent of GDP, other Southeast Asian countries were maintaining healthier, more moderate surpluses of less than 1 percent of GDP (*The Economist*, 2007).

Foreign multinational corporations primarily conduct Southeast Asia's trade with the Western industrialized economies. Historically, the region's companies, including those of the New Asian Emperors, have emphasized a regional thrust to their developmental and trade ties. At first, the regional companies' small size hindered their efforts in international competition. The region's growth and market opportunities also attracted the interest and investment of regional companies, as well as presenting them with opportunities. An example is the growth triangle negotiated by Singapore, Malaysia's state of Johor, and Indonesia's Riau Islands, which has served as a focus for economic growth and investment. Consequently, though Southeast Asian companies investing in the West's industrialized, information-rich economies gain advantages of abundant information when they do so, they have to deal with the informational void of their own region in conducting the great majority of their business operations in what they consider their primary markets.

As we identified in other research (Haley, Haley, and Tan, 2004), increasingly the Overseas Chinese are also encountering the People's Republic of China's complex tri-network informational void as they increase their exports and business with that country. Very simply, the Overseas Chinese often lack the time necessary to cultivate and use most effectively the PRC's three networks of business, government/Chinese Communist Party, and family. As Edward Zeng, CEO of Sparkice, told us, "To be truly successful today, you must be able to build and call on relationships in all three networks" (Haley, Haley, and Tan, 2004, p. 99).

The informational void, especially regarding the external environment of firms operating in the region, determines the strategic management style and procedures of Southeast Asia's Overseas Chinese. The informational void also poses a serious challenge to traditional forms of strategic planning and management that senior executives and managers employ in the industrialized countries' information-rich economies. As we showed in the previous chapter, Western multinationals entering Southeast Asia cannot expect their Overseas Chinese competitors and potential strategic partners to behave as the Japanese do.

Specifically, the region presents Western multinationals with a substantial challenge to their traditional, information-rich, strategic-management techniques. We have argued (Haley, Haley, and Tan, 2004) that Chinese companies' management, including those of the Overseas Chinese, are developing Western-style professional management skills while retaining the best aspects of traditional management. Yet Western managers appear more dependent than ever before on readily available, massive amounts of data and information. As Ayres (2007) noted, the larger and more massive databases in the West have assumed increasing importance for managerial decision making. In a similar vein, a March 2008 study by data-storage giant EMC reported that digital data in Asia will grow at a compound annual rate of 57 percent between 2006 and 2010, to reach 1.8 zettabytes (1,800 billion gigabytes). According to the study, estimated data volume will exceed total available storage space by nearly 50 percent. The EMC stated that in 2008, Singapore alone will create more than 1,200 terabytes of digital information. EMC expected the data explosion to affect most directly industries such as health care, telecommunications, and finance, which are expanding their storage capacity in anticipation of the expected growth in digital data (Yeo, 2008). However, the digital-data explosion within Southeast Asian companies has not translated into information on their strategic operations that companies have released or plan to release. Indeed, our research shows that companies and governments continue to contribute to the informational void in Asia.

First, using information that Western theorists have generally considered desirable for strategic decisions, we delineate the extent and characteristics of the informational void in Southeast Asia. We present evidence of the Southeast Asian informational void (which we describe as a black hole), both before and after the financial crisis, and compare the available information with that in the U.S. Next, drawing on our interviews with CEOs of Overseas Chinese companies (some of whom we identify in the Appendix), we show how their decision-making styles have adapted to the informational void. In the final section, we present some thoughts on and reasons for the bolstering of Southeast Asia's informational void.

The Informational Black Hole of Southeast Asia

Tables 4.1 and 4.2 present the results of a literature search of the ABI-Inform database, probably the most commonly available

TABLE 4.1: *Academic Articles on Southeast Asia*

	Brunei				Myanmar				Cambodia				Indonesia				Laos			
Period*	1	2	3	4	1	2	3	4	1	2	3	4	1	2	3	4	1	2	3	4
Topic																				
Marketing	0	0	0	0	0	0	0	0	0	1	0	0	1	8	2	5	0	1	0	1
Pricing	0	0	0	0	0	0	0	0	0	0	0	0	0	3	1	7	0	0	0	0
Promotion	0	0	0	0	0	0	0	0	0	0	0	0	0	0	0	2	0	0	0	0
Distribution	0	1	0	0	0	0	0	0	0	1	0	0	1	1	2	0	0	1	0	1
Product development	0	0	0	0	0	0	0	0	0	0	0	0	0	0	1	0	0	0	0	0
Channels	0	0	0	0	0	0	0	0	0	0	0	0	0	0	0	0	0	0	0	1
Buyer behavior	0	0	0	0	0	0	0	0	0	0	0	0	0	0	0	0	0	0	0	0
Consumer behavior	0	0	0	1	0	0	0	0	0	0	0	0	0	2	0	0	0	0	0	0
Demographics	0	0	0	0	0	0	0	0	0	0	0	4	1	1	0	10	0	0	0	0
Advertising	0	0	0	0	0	0	0	0	0	0	0	0	0	2	0	3	0	0	0	0
Product management	0	0	0	0	0	0	0	0	0	0	0	0	0	0	0	0	0	0	0	0
Sales management	0	0	0	0	0	0	0	0	0	0	0	0	0	0	0	0	0	0	0	0
In-store	0	0	0	0	0	0	0	0	0	0	0	0	0	0	0	0	0	0	0	0
Business research	0	0	0	0	0	0	0	0	0	0	0	0	0	0	0	2	0	0	0	0
Management research	0	0	0	0	0	0	0	0	0	0	0	0	0	0	0	0	0	0	0	0
Market research	0	0	0	0	0	0	0	0	0	0	0	0	0	0	1	2	0	0	0	0
Consumer research	0	0	0	0	0	0	0	0	0	0	0	0	0	0	0	0	0	0	0	0

(continued)

TABLE 4.1 (Continued)

	Brunei				Myanmar				Cambodia				Indonesia				Laos			
Period*	1	2	3	4	1	2	3	4	1	2	3	4	1	2	3	4	1	2	3	4
Industrial marketing	0	0	0		0	0	0	0	0	0	0	0	0	2	0	1	0	0	0	0
Transportation/logistics	0	0	0	0	0	0	0	1	0	0	0	0	2	0	1	2	0	0	0	2
Strategic management	0	0	0	0	0	0	0	0	0	0	0	0	0	1	0	2	0	0	0	0
Management decision making	0	0	0	0	0	0	0	0	0	0	0	0	0	0	0	0	0	0	0	0
Culture	1	1	0	1	0	0	0	1	0	0	0	2	1	4	1	37	0	0	0	1
Media habits	0	0	0	2	0	0	0	0	0	0	0	0	0	0	0	0	0	0	0	0
Mass communications	0	0	0	0	0	0	0	0	0	0	0	0	0	0	0	4	0	0	0	0
Strategic planning	0	0	0	0	0	0	0	0	0	0	0	0	0	2	0	3	0	0	0	0
Total ACA	1	2	0	4	0	0	0	2	0	2	0	6	6	26	9	80	0	2	0	6

	Malaysia				Philippines				Singapore				Thailand				Vietnam			
Period*	1	2	3	4	1	2	3	4	1	2	3	4	1	2	3	4	1	2	3	4
Topic																				
Marketing	3	5	9	45	0	1	0	8	9	13	11	41	3	11	5	30	0	1	0	12
Pricing	2	2	1	5	0	0	0	3	2	1	0	21	0	0	1	5	0	0	0	1
Promotion	0	0	0	7	0	0	0	2	2	2	3	5	0	0	0	3	0	0	0	1
Distribution	2	2	5	3	0	0	0	2	1	10	1	4	1	2	2	5	0	1	1	2
Product development	0	0	0	3	0	0	0	0	1	0	1	6	0	1	0	6	0	0	0	0
Channels	0	0	0	1	0	0	0	1	0	0	0	0	0	1	0	1	0	0	0	0
Buyer behavior	0	0	0	0	0	0	0	0	0	0	0	0	0	0	0	0	0	0	0	1

(continued)

TABLE 4.1 (Continued)

	Malaysia				Philippines				Singapore				Thailand				Vietnam			
	1	2	3	4	1	2	3	4	1	2	3	4	1	2	3	4	1	2	3	4
Consumer behavior	1	0	0	22	0	0	0	1	2	3	2	23	0	4	1	7	0	0	0	7
Demographics	7	2	3	9	0	0	0	6	4	2	2	11	2	2	1	8	0	0	0	3
Advertising	1	3	2	7	0	0	0	1	2	2	5	10	0	2	1	9	0	0	0	3
Product management	0	0	0	0	0	0	0	0	0	0	0	0	0	0	0	1	0	0	0	0
Sales management	0	0	0	2	0	0	0	0	0	0	0	0	0	0	0	0	0	0	0	0
In-store	0	0	0	0	0	0	0	0	0	0	0	0	0	0	0	0	0	0	0	0
Business research	0	0	0	0	0	0	0	0	0	0	0	0	0	1	1	0	0	0	0	3
Management research	0	0	0	0	0	0	0	0	0	0	0	1	0	0	0	1	0	0	0	0
Market research	0	0	2	0	0	0	0	3	5	1	4	1	0	0	1	3	0	0	0	1
Consumer research	0	0	0	1	0	0	0	0	1	1	0	0	0	1	0	4	0	0	0	0
Industrial marketing	0	0	0	3	0	0	0	1	0	0	0	2	0	0	0	4	0	0	1	1
Transportation/logistics	3	1	0	5	0	0	0	2	5	3	1	15	2	1	2	8	0	0	0	8
Strategic management	0	1	0	7	0	0	0	2	0	3	0	19	0	1	0	2	0	0	0	3
Management decision making	0	0	0	3	0	0	0	0	0	1	0	6	0	0	0	0	0	0	0	1
Culture	1	2	2	24	0	0	0	7	5	11	9	77	2	6	7	33	0	0	1	12
Media habits	0	0	0	0	0	0	0	0	0	0	0	0	0	0	0	0	0	0	0	0
Mass communication	0	0	0	4	0	0	0	1	0	0	1	3	0	0	0	1	0	1	0	5
Strategic planning	1	3	1	7	0	0	0	2	0	7	9	9	0	3	0	5	0	0	1	3
Total ACA	21	21	25	159	0	1	0	42	39	60	49	254	9	36	20	136	0	3	4	67

Note: *Periods: 1 = 1587–1989, 2 = 1990–1993, 3 = 1994 to mid-1995, 4 = 2001–2007.

TABLE 4.2: *Business Articles on Southeast Asia*

	Brunei				Myanmar				Cambodia				Indonesia				Laos			
Period*	1	2	3	4	1	2	3	4	1	2	3	4	1	2	3	4	1	2	3	4
Topic																				
Marketing	0	0	0	0	0	1	0	2	0	1	0	0	3	39	36	5	0	2	0	1
Pricing	0	0	0	0	1	0	0	0	0	0	1	0	1	4	1	4	0	0	2	1
Promotion	0	0	0	0	0	0	0	0	0	0	0	0	0	2	0	1	0	0	0	1
Distribution	1	2	0	0	0	0	0	0	0	1	1	0	2	20	11	5	0	1	1	1
Product development	0	0	0	0	0	0	0	0	0	1	1	0	0	5	3	3	0	0	0	0
Channels	0	0	0	0	0	0	0	0	0	0	0	0	0	0	0	0	0	0	0	0
Buyer behavior	0	0	0	0	0	0	0	0	0	0	0	0	0	0	0	0	0	0	0	0
Consumer behavior	0	0	0	0	0	1	1	0	0	0	1	0	1	4	0	0	0	0	1	0
Demographics	0	0	0	0	0	0	0	1	0	0	0	2	2	6	0	2	0	0	0	0
Advertising	0	0	1	0	0	1	2	3	0	0	1	0	0	15	5	25	0	2	1	0
Product management	0	0	0	0	0	0	0	0	0	0	0	0	0	0	0	0	0	0	0	0
Sales management	0	0	0	0	0	0	0	0	0	0	0	0	0	0	0	0	0	0	0	0
In-store	0	0	0	0	0	0	0	0	0	0	0	0	0	0	0	0	0	0	0	0
Business research	0	0	0	0	0	0	0	0	0	0	0	0	1	0	0	3	0	0	0	0
Management research	0	0	0	0	0	0	0	0	0	0	0	0	0	0	0	0	0	0	0	0
Market research	0	0	0	0	0	0	0	0	0	0	0	0	0	1	1	1	0	0	0	0
Consumer research	0	0	0	0	0	0	0	0	0	0	0	0	0	0	0	0	0	0	0	0

(continued)

TABLE 4.2 (Continued)

	Brunei				Myanmar				Cambodia				Indonesia				Laos			
	1	2	3	4	1	2	3	4	1	2	3	4	1	2	3	4	1	2	3	4
Industrial marketing	0	0	0	0	0	0	0	0	0	0	0	0	0	3	0	5	0	0	0	0
Transportation/logistics	0	0	0	0	0	0	0	4	0	1	0	2	5	19	10	13	0	1	2	2
Strategic management	0	0	0	0	0	0	0	0	0	0	0	0	0	1	0	2	0	0	2	0
Management decision making	0	0	0	0	0	0	0	0	0	0	0	0	0	0	0	1	0	0	0	0
Culture	1	1	1	0	0	1	0	1	0	0	0	3	1	9	6	49	0	4	1	1
Media habits	0	0	0	0	0	0	0	0	0	0	0	0	0	0	0	2	0	0	0	0
Mass communication	0	0	0	0	0	1	0	0	0	0	0	0	0	0	0	1	0	1	0	1
Strategic planning	0	1	0	1	0	0	0	0	0	0	0	0	0	8	1	10	0	0	0	0
Total articles	2	4	2	1	5	3	11		0	3	4	7	16	136	74	132	0	11	10	8

	Malaysia				Philippines				Singapore				Thailand				Vietnam			
Period*	1	2	3	4	1	2	3	4	1	2	3	4	1	2	3	4	1	2	3	4
Topic																				
Marketing	16	61	32	134	0	1	0	320	20	21	16	115	6	23	12	55	0	10	17	5
Pricing	5	7	5	24	0	0	0	35	3	2	1	15	1	6	1	8	0	2	1	3
Promotion	0	1	8	44	0	0	0	133	4	5	3	9	2	1	0	14	0	0	1	1
Distribution	8	22	9	19	0	0	0	95	5	18	3	16	6	8	6	16	0	1	6	10
Product development	2	5	0	10	0	0	0	11	1	3	5	5	0	2	0	3	0	1	0	0
Channels	0	0	0	7	0	0	0	10	0	0	0	2	1	2	0	1	0	1	0	0
Buyer behavior	0	0	0	0	0	0	0	0	0	0	0	0	0	0	0	0	0	0	0	0
Consumer behavior	1	2	0	4	0	0	0	4	2	4	3	7	0	7	2	7	0	0	1	2
Demographics	7	4	3	9	0	0	0	18	5	6	2	5	2	6	2	5	0	1	1	2

(continued)

TABLE 4.2 (*Continued*)

	Malaysia				Philippines				Singapore				Thailand				Vietnam			
Advertising	5	11	6	168	0	0	0	144	5	10	16	256	2	12	5	78	0	7	10	25
Product management	0	1	0	0	0	0	0	0	0	0	0	1	0	0	0	0	0	0	0	0
Sales management	0	0	0	0	0	0	0	0	0	0	0	2	0	0	0	1	0	0	0	0
In-store	0	0	0	0	0	0	0	0	0	0	0	0	0	0	0	0	0	1	0	0
Business research	0	0	0	0	0	0	0	1	0	0	0	0	0	1	1	0	0	0	0	0
Management research	0	0	0	0	0	0	0	0	0	0	0	0	0	0	0	0	0	0	0	0
Market research	0	0	2	2	0	0	0	4	5	2	4	8	0	1	1	2	0	0	0	2
Consumer research	0	0	0	1	0	0	0	0	1	1	0	1	0	1	0	0	0	0	0	0
Industrial marketing	0	0	0	5	0	0	0	2	0	0	0	3	0	0	0	1	0	2	2	0
Transportation/logistics	6	5	9	41	0	0	1	141	10	21	7	133	5	10	9	37	1	4	14	27
Strategic management	0	1	0	5	0	0	0	2	0	4	0	4	0	1	0	2	0	0	0	2
Management decision making	0	0	0	1	0	0	0	1	0	1	0	2	0	0	0	0	0	0	0	0
Culture	2	9	9	15	0	0	0	74	5	17	13	25	5	12	13	11	0	3	4	4
Media habits	0	0	0	1	0	0	0	2	0	0	0	2	0	0	0	1	0	0	0	0
Mass communication	0	1	0	3	0	0	0	29	0	0	1	2	0	1	1	5	0	2	0	3
Strategic planning	1	6	7	9	0	0	0	8	1	17	9	16	3	11	3	3	0	1	4	4
Total articles	53	136	90	502	0	1	1	1,034	67	126	83	629	33	105	56	250	1	36	61	90

*Note: * Periods: 1 = 1987–1989, 2 = 1990–1993, 3 = 1994 to mid-1995, 4 = 2004–2007.*

database of published articles worldwide. To ascertain the historical evolution of the black hole, we looked for strategic data in four information periods: 1987–1989, 1990–1993, 1994 to mid-1995, and finally the post-crises period of 2004–2007.

Four methodological issues in our study (Haley and Tan, 1996) need elaboration. First, each topic title represents three or four topical keyword searches. For example, "market research" represents searches we conducted using the keywords *marketing research, market research, market data*, and *marketing data*. The keywords represent many of the kinds of information that strategic planners and executives use to understand their environment when they plan.

Second, we screened the results in Tables 4.1 and 4.2 to eliminate spurious hits unrelated to management issues and ensure that the articles addressed the subject matter, or its application, in the countries we searched. The most common problem of this sort related to Vietnam, where many articles profiling particular U.S. executives or firms mentioned the executives as Vietnam War veterans or the firm's Vietnam War–related activities; however, strategic planners rarely consider these factors as important, and we eliminated such hits from the two tables.

Third, we conducted the research only on the 10 ASEAN (Association of Southeast Asian Nations) countries; yet all available evidence indicates that we can generalize our results to Taiwan despite its size, importance, and level of development.

Finally, though our database has a Western (even an English-language) bias, this bias remains consistent over the entire period of the study. Alternatively, Southeast Asia's relative economic importance to the West has increased over the period this study covered. Though most Western media have focused on the economic performance of the PRC and India in recent years, Southeast Asia has shown resurgent importance. For example, costs in China have risen to where investment is returning to Southeast Asia, and Vietnam constitutes the second-fastest-growing economy in the world, with its GDP having doubled between 1991 and 2000 (Neupert, Baughn, and Dao, 2005). Thus, despite our study's inherent regional and linguistic biases, if articles by business authors and researchers reflect the relative economic importance of the region, coverage of Southeast Asian markets should have increased relative to coverage of the U.S. markets or to total articles worldwide.

In our data and tables, the phrase *academic articles* refers to those published in refereed business and economics journals; *business articles* refers to those published in the popular press, newspapers, and general-interest business magazines. We use the term *total articles*, or simply *articles*, to refer to the combination of both categories.

Ironically, the results across all four time periods revealed that academic researchers tended to concentrate on Singapore, the smallest state geographically in the region, with the second-smallest population, and one of the smallest regional economies. In the post-crises period 2004–2007, despite exhortations for more information on the region's business operations and competitive environment, the situation remained essentially the same. The Philippines had the most total articles, because of articles in the business press, not by academic researchers. Singapore once again dominated among articles by academic researchers with more than 100 research articles published on Singapore beyond the number for the next most-heavily researched country. Although Singapore has the region's wealthiest, most advanced economy and domestic market structure, it also probably has the most homogenized and Westernized business community and environment outside North America, Western Europe, Australia, or New Zealand.

Table 4.3 compares the Southeast Asian, Taiwanese, and U.S. markets in population, GDP, and geographic size. The table shows that Southeast Asia's GDP, at US$3.3 billion, represents 23.8 percent of the U.S. economy's US$13.9 billion. Southeast Asia also has a significantly smaller land mass, representing only 47.5 percent of

TABLE 4.3: *Comparing Southeast Asia and Taiwan to the U.S.*

	Population [a]	GDP (Billions[b])	Area (Sq. Mi.)
Brunei	374,577	9.6[c]	2,226
Burma	47,374,000	91.1[d]	261,228
Cambodia	13,996,000	25.8[d]	70,238
Indonesia	234,694,000	845.6[d]	741,052
Laos	6,522,000	12.6[d]	91,429
Malaysia	24,821,000	357.9[d]	127,584
Philippines	91,077,000	298.9[d]	115,860
Singapore	4,553,000	222.7[d]	247
Thailand	65,068,000	519.9[d]	198,115
Vietnam	85,262,000	222.5[d]	127,246
Taiwan	22,859,000	690.1[d]	13,892
Total	596,600,577	3,296.7	1,749,117
United States	301,140,000	13,860.0[d]	3,679,192
Comparison, total to the U.S.	198.1%	23.8%	47.5%

Notes: [a] U.S. Census Bureau, world population estimates, midyear 2007; [b] CIA World Fact Book, in U.S. dollars at purchasing power parity; [c] 2006 estimate; [d] 2007 estimate.

the U.S. land mass. But the region has a considerably larger population, almost 200 percent that of the U.S.

Figure 4.1 shows that even though little information exists on Southeast Asia, what there is has increased sharply. For adequate strategic planning in the U.S., Western firms often gather and analyze specific data relating to market segments; various corporate and societal cultures; and myriad economic, competitive, political, and legal environments. These data assume far more complexity for Southeast Asia. The U.S. arguably constitutes the most culturally diverse nation in the world; however, its legal, political, and economic environments vary little across states. By contrast, each country in Southeast Asia has its own rich historical, cultural, linguistic,

FIGURE 4.1: *Average Annual Articles on Southeast Asia, 1987–2007*

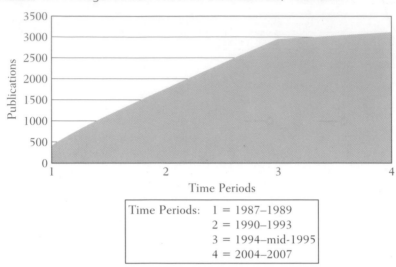

Time Periods: 1 = 1987–1989
2 = 1990–1993
3 = 1994–mid-1995
4 = 2004–2007

economic, legal, and ethnic backgrounds. Of the 11 nations, only Thailand escaped colonialism. Thus, Southeast Asian countries exhibit myriad differences in local cultures originating from their diverse histories and populations. Given the region's inherent complexity, the research and publication on the region seems exceedingly small.

To gauge changes over time, we compared the number of articles on Southeast Asia with those for the U.S. and the total number of articles the database held for the search topics regardless of geographic limitations. Today, sparse appropriate data and market information remains a problem, and investors can expect this problem in some markets for years to come (Tucker, 2007).

Table 4.4 indicates the imbalance in the relative number of articles on the U.S. and Southeast Asia. Looking from Table 4.4A through 4.4B and 4.4C to 4.4D, we notice the increase in articles on Southeast Asia from one time period to the next. Table 4.4D in particular shows a substantial increase in the number of articles on Southeast Asia. However, total articles and articles on the U.S. have

TABLE 4.4A: *Southeast Asia Articles Trends: Period 1, 1987–1989*

Topic	Southeast Asia			U.S. Number	Total on Topic
	Number	% of U.S.	% of Total		
Marketing	79	2.9	.56	2,681	14,012
Pricing	16	2.6	.48	612	3,367
Promotion	20	3.4	.66	585	3,037
Distribution	37	2.6	.55	1,416	6,710
Product development	5	0.9	.22	505	2,306
Channels of distribution	4	3.1	.64	130	626
Buyer behavior	0	0.0	.00	1	13
Consumer behavior	3	1.5	.23	196	1,280
Demographics	15	2.4	.76	629	1,983
Advertising	22	1.6	.36	1,390	6,070
Product management	0	0.0	.00	29	226
Sales management	0	0.0	.00	15	222
Point-of-purchase	1	1.8	.27	56	370
Business research/data	2	3.7	.64	54	311
Management research/data	0	0.0	.00	16	288
Market research/data	11	13.1	.35	84	3,183
Consumer research/data	1	4.3	.44	23	228
Business-to-business	1	1.1	.14	87	697
Transportation/logistics	31	4.4	1.14	698	2,715
Strategic management	1	2.5	.28	40	357
Management decision making	0	0.0	.00	13	118
Culture	30	4.7	1.14	645	2,642
Media habits	0	0.0	.00	4	13
Mass media/communication	1	4.2	.86	24	116
Strategic planning	15	2.4	.43	632	3,528
Totals	1,391	4.9		28,443	

TABLE 4.4B: *Southeast Asia Articles Trends: Period 2, 1990–1993*

Topic	Southeast Asia			U.S. Number	Total on Topic
	Number	% of U.S.	% of Total		
Marketing	219	1.0	.75	21,174	29,297
Pricing	41	0.9	.63	4,661	6,530
Promotion	76	1.9	1.35	4,100	5,648
Distribution	117	1.3	.88	8,739	13,271
Product development	32	0.6	.47	5,321	6,852
Channels of distribution	10	1.4	1.00	725	999
Buyer behavior	0	0.0	.00	21	31
Consumer behavior	17	1.2	.71	1,474	2,387
Demographics	25	0.9	.73	2,789	3,422
Advertising	73	0.6	.46	13,164	15,984
Product management	1	0.5	.34	186	298
Sales management	0	0.0	.00	195	260
Point-of-purchase	2	0.3	.25	685	812
Business research/data	1	0.2	.13	442	787
Management research/data	0	0.0	.00	212	491
Market research/data	19	0.7	.39	2,789	4,828
Consumer research/data	19	10.4	5.54	183	343
Business-to-business	8	1.1	.78	721	1,021
Transportation/logistics	83	1.8	1.12	4726	7,406
Strategic management	5	1.0	.61	482	826
Management decision making	1	1.2	.65	83	154
Culture	111	3.0	1.81	3,707	6,142
Media habits	0	0.0	.00	20	30
Mass media/communication	2	0.9	.68	226	296
Strategic planning	162	2.4	1.57	6,784	10,320
Totals	5,444	2.5		216,016	

TABLE 4.4C: *Southeast Asia Articles Trends: Period 3, 1994 to Mid-1995*

Topic	Southeast Asia Num.	% of U.S.	% of Total	U.S. Number	Total on Topic
Marketing	155	1.0	.65	15,739	23,766
Pricing	29	1.0	.77	2,894	3,750
Promotion	60	2.3	1.63	2,647	3,672
Distribution	63	1.0	.73	6,472	8,683
Product development	17	0.3	.34	4,974	4,974
Channels of distribution	4	0.5	.42	845	958
Buyer behavior	0	0.0	.00	11	14
Consumer behavior	9	1.0	.70	867	1,292
Demographics	10	0.6	.55	1,573	1,826
Advertising	60	0.5	.36	11,461	16,490
Product management	0	0.0	.00	109	153
Sales management	0	0.0	.00	254	280
Point-of-purchase	2	0.4	.37	457	545
Business research/data	3	1.1	.76	262	393
Management research/data	1	0.6	.29	179	350
Market research/data	11	0.7	.11	1,512	2,483
Consumer research/data	0	0.0	.00	108	156
Business-to-business	7	1.4	1.13	483	620
Transportation/logistics	64	1.9	1.29	3,361	4,978
Strategic management	1	0.3	.21	324	477
Management decision making	0	0.0	.00	32	53
Culture	91	3.6	2.39	2,521	3,808
Media habits	0	0.0	.00	8	11
Mass media/communication	2	1.5	.89	134	225
Strategic planning	83	1.3	1.02	6,197	8,126
Totals	4,430	2.3		189,610	

TABLE 4.4D: *Southeast Asia Articles Trends: Period 4, 2004–2007*

Topic	Southeast Asia Number	% of U.S.	% of Total	U.S. Number	Total on Topic
Marketing	779	1.4	.39	55,592	202,305
Pricing	132	1.1	.46	11,781	28,737
Promotion	223	2.8	.83	8,019	26,807
Distribution	179	0.8	.27	23,343	65,612
Product development	47	0.5	.24	9,992	19,267
Channels of distribution	24	0.9	.44	2,823	5,405
Buyer behavior	1	4.8	1.37	21	73
Consumer behavior	85	2.0	.90	4,186	9,411
Demographics	93	1.7	.85	5,377	10,969
Advertising	734	2.0	.88	36,333	83,382
Product management	2	0.4	.13	572	1,571
Sales management	6	0.4	.31	1,344	1,936
Point-of-purchase	0	0.0	.00	210	491
Business research/data	9	0.8	.54	487	1,657
Management research/data	2	0.4	.10	459	1,960
Market research/data	29	0.5	.21	5,929	13,809
Consumer research/data	7	1.1	.45	610	1,551
Business-to-business	28	0.9	.45	2,997	6,206
Transportation/logistics	443	2.1	.58	20,671	75,961
Strategic management	52	1.0	.47	5,322	10,662
Management decision making	15	3.7	1.15	406	1,306
Culture	384	2.5	.90	15,647	42,878
Media habits	8	20.0	9.76	39	82
Mass media/communication	62	9.3	2.76	669	2,244
Strategic planning	80	0.9	.50	8,676	15,967
Totals	9,420	4.3		221,475	

also increased substantially.[1] The combined increases confound our ability to determine whether the increased articles on Southeast Asia represent a greater proportion of articles covering the region; that would reflect the region's increasing economic and political importance. If a greater proportion does not exist, the larger number probably reflects only an increase in articles that ABI-Inform tracked.

Table 4.4E presents a signs test for the first three, pre-crises time periods. By taking the percentages for articles listed in Tables 4.4A, 4.4B, and 4.4A, and subtracting them from the percentages in Tables 4.4B, 4.4C, and 4.4C, respectively, one gets a series of positive (+), negative (-), or no change (/) results. A signs test can then determine if an actual increase in articles has occurred relative to the U.S. and to total articles for the topics. If articles on Southeast Asia have continued to increase significantly, relative to the U.S. or to total articles, plus (positive) signs should dominate; if not, minus (negative) signs or slash (no-change) signs should dominate. Perfect chance would be represented by an equal number of plus and minus signs. A Z-score can then determine if the variance from chance is significant. The data for period 4 is shown in Table 4.4D, and the signs test for period 4 versus the first three periods is shown in Table 4.4F.

In considering Table 4.4E, we see that plus signs did not dominate articles in pre-crisis Southeast Asia; most signs emerge negative when comparing articles on Southeast Asia with articles on the U.S. In testing the Z-score for plus signs, we found that the negative trend runs extensively and deeply. Even after the widespread drop in articles from period 1 (1987–1989) to period 2 (1990–1993), the drop between period 2 and period 3 (1994–1995) remained significant at the 0.06 level.

---

[1] The base of information in Table 4.4 differs from that of Tables 4.1 and 4.2. The enormous number of articles on the U.S. for some topic areas exceeded our ability to screen them as we did for Tables 4.1 and 4.2. To ensure comparability, Table 4.4 uses unscreened totals for articles from Southeast Asia as well.

TABLE 4.4E: *The Signs Test for Pre-crisis Articles on Southeast Asia (1987–1995)*

Topic	Compared to U.S.			Compared to Topic Total		
	B - A	C - B	C - A	B - A	C - B	C - A
Marketing	−	/	−	+	−	+
Pricing	−	+	−	+	+	+
Promotion	−	+	−	+	+	+
Distribution	−	−	−	+	−	+
Product development	−	−	−	+	−	+
Channels of distribution	−	−	−	+	−	−
Buyer behavior	/	/	/	/	/	/
Consumer behavior	−	−	−	+	−	+
Demographics	−	−	−	−	−	−
Advertising	−	−	−	+	−	/
Product management	+	−	/	+	−	/
Sales management	/	/	/	/	/	/
Point-of-purchase	−	+	−	−	+	+
Business research/data	−	+	+	−	+	+
Management research/data	/	+	−	/	+	+
Market research/data	−	/	−	+	+	+
Consumer research/data	+	−	+	−	−	−
Business-to-business	/	+	−	+	+	+
Transportation/logistics	−	+	−	−	+	+
Strategic management	−	−	/	+	−	−
Management decision making	+	−	−	+	−	/
Culture	−	+	/	+	+	+
Media habits	/	/	−	/	/	/
Mass media/communication	−	+	−	−	/	+
Strategic planning	/	−	−	+	−	+
Total on region	−	−	−			
Number of pluses	3	9	2	15	9	15
Z-scores for + signs	−3.92	−1.57	−4.31	1.41	−1.98	1.41
Probability	000	0.058	0.000	0.079	0.024	0.079
Number of minuses	17	12	19	6	12	4
Z-scores for - signs	1.57	−0.39	2.35	−3.68	−0.28	−5.72
Probability	0.058	0.348	0.009	0.000	0.390	0.000

Though the second score does not produce the strongest endorsement, considering the drop in the number of plus signs between the first two periods it remains significant. Because plus and minus are not mutually exclusive, and because a substantial number of *no change* occur in our middle column, we conducted a second signs test for minus signs. Here, we found that changes between periods 1 and 2 assume significance only at the .06 level, and that changes between periods 2 and 3 have no significance at all. Changes between the beginning and end of the time periods we studied showed that the negative trend in coverage is highly significant. In Table 4.4F, the signs test for period 4, the years 2004–2007, we see that, although more plus signs emerge, a significant relationship exists only between period 4 and period 3, the pre-crisis years 1994 to mid-1995. Period 3 had the least coverage of Southeast Asia. When one compares post-crisis period 4 with the pre-crisis period exhibiting the greatest coverage of Southeast Asia, period 1, a negative relationship emerges at a relatively strong, but not yet significant, level. Thus, we can conclude that relative to the U.S., Southeast Asia remains an informational black hole for readily available data and research even after the 1997 financial crisis.

In the pre-crisis years, shown in Table 4.4E, comparison of articles on Southeast Asia with total articles on the topics shows that the region fared better. Overall, a trend of increased coverage on Southeast Asia has occurred relative to total articles. Interestingly, both the overall increase, as measured by the number of pluses, and the increase between period 1 and period 2, as measured by the number of pluses, are significant only at the .08 level, and virtually all of the overall increase comes initially (to period 2 from period 1). In comparing the change in articles between periods 2 and 3, we find that the number of pluses falls significantly below chance (at the .02 level). Though none of the analyses show the number of minuses above the chance level (12.5 in this instance), they would seem to indicate that the 1990s saw a leveling off, or perhaps even some reduction, in the relative number of articles published on Southeast Asia. This trend occurred regardless of the

TABLE 4.4F: *The Signs Test for Post-crisis Articles on Southeast Asia (2004–2007)*

Topic	Compared to U.S.			Compared to Topic Total		
	D – A	D – B	D – C	D – A	D – B	D – C
Marketing	–	+	+	–	–	–
Pricing	–	+	+	–	–	–
Promotion	–	+	+	+	–	–
Distribution	–	–	–	–	–	–
Product development	–	–	+	+	–	–
Channels of distribution	–	–	+	–	–	+
Buyer behavior	+	+	+	+	+	+
Consumer behavior	+	+	+	+	+	+
Demographics	–	+	+	+	+	+
Advertising	+	+	+	+	+	+
Product management	+	–	+	+	–	+
Sales management	+	+	+	+	+	+
Point-of-purchase	–	–	–	–	–	–
Business research/data	–	+	+	–	+	–
Management research/data	+	+	–	+	+	–
Market research/data	–	–	–	–	–	–
Consumer research/data	–	–	+	+	–	+
Business-to-business	–	–	–	+	–	–
Transportation/logistics	–	+	+	–	–	–
Strategic management	+	/	+	+	–	+
Management decision making	+	+	+	–	+	+
Culture	–	–	–	–	–	–
Media habits	+	+	+	+	+	+
Mass media/communication	+	+	+	+	+	+
Strategic planning	–	–	–	+	–	–
Total on region	–	+	–			
Number of pluses	10	15	18	15	10	12
Z-scores for + signs	−1.18	0.78	1.96	1.41	−1.41	− 0.28
Probability	0.119	0.218	0.025	0.079	0.079	0.390
Number of minuses	16	10	8	10	15	13
Z-scores for - signs	1.18	−1.18	−1.96	−1.41	1.41	0.28
Probability	0.119	0.119	0.025	0.079	0.079	0.390

much greater interest the private sector showed in the area through its investment in the region. With increasing foreign investment in the region aimed at serving local markets, rather than markets in the industrialized countries, the overall trend in research and articles is puzzling. Shifting forward to Table 4.4F to consider more recent trends, we see that none of the relationships were significant at the .05 level, but there was a slightly negative trend, with the relationship between period 4 and period 1 being positive, showing greater coverage of Southeast Asia, but turning negative compared to period 2, and continuing on a slightly negative trend compared to period 3. Once again, the analysis comparing Southeast Asia with overall worldwide articles on the topics indicates continuation of the informational black hole in Southeast Asia.

In more recent times, the trend for articles and information on Southeast Asia has continued to mystify. Given the two crises that hit Southeast Asia, and in particular the SARS crisis, which ended just before period 4, together with the continued economic importance of the region, one would have expected coverage of the region to have increased, not to have muddled along the same path. The informational black hole appears to have placed finite limits on the research and coverage of non-U.S. markets.

Analysis indicates that Southeast Asia as a region continues to constitute an informational void. The tables also show that the more industrially developed nations in the region, such as Singapore, generated more articles than the less industrially developed ones, regardless of the relative size of the markets. This emerged as especially true when considering articles by academics. Surprisingly, post-crisis articles on the Philippines have skyrocketed. Indeed, without the articles on the Philippines, articles on Southeast Asia in 2004–2007 would have dropped dramatically. Generally, information on any country does not correspond with its stage of economic development. Consequently, the level of relative economic development does not explain adequately the informational black hole of Southeast Asia. However, the Philippines was once a U.S. colony, and this is one of the few factors distinguishing the country from other Southeast Asian countries. This historical relationship, and the resultant comfort level, leads to a possible explanation for the large number of articles on the Philippines vis-à-vis other Southeast Asian countries.

The next section describes the changes in management style that the black hole of Southeast Asia has produced.

Operating in an Informational Black Hole

We can better understand the development and maintenance of the informational black hole through an additional aspect of the history of business development in the region: interactions between the major types of regional businesses. Southeast Asia has historically had three major clusters of large businesses: state-owned or government-linked corporations (GLCs), the Overseas Chinese family businesses, and multinational corporations. Recently, other clusters have arisen, notably the Overseas Indian family businesses and indigenous business groups (such as Malaysia's *bumiputras*, from the Sanskrit for "sons of the soil"). All groups have prospered through operating in the informational void, for various reasons. The groups, rather than insisting that the environment conform to traditional strategic-management perceptions of desirable data, chose to adjust their strategies and management accordingly and coped quite adequately with their environments. They had differing reasons and needs, but they achieved similar end results.

We first consider the GLCs. These organizations have played a major role in the development of many industries in their home countries and, have in some instances, contributed a great deal to their national economic development. Few are actually government-owned, but they are usually started as suppliers of products or services in a protected, if not monopolistic, domestic market environment. With strong domestic demand caused by the tremendous economic growth in the region, and lack of serious competition, many of these businesses flourished; many others evolved into inefficient dinosaurs kept in apparently good health by the region's economy more than anything else. For such businesses, their countries' plans for economic growth and development dictated their strategic-planning and management patterns. Hence, market information and industry data never constituted critical success factors. Many believed that the 1997 Asian financial crisis would provoke reforms in this area; it did not. For example, Young (2002) found that the close links between Southeast Asia's GLCs and family-owned companies and their governments have continued unabated.

We next consider the foreign multinationals, which generally arrived in the region much later than the Overseas Chinese. European trading houses have existed for decades in Southeast Asia. Indeed, many of the old European international trading houses have longer pedigrees in Asia than the Overseas Chinese companies. However, the trading houses did not shape Southeast Asian business environments as much as did the manufacturing-based multinationals that entered the region in large numbers much more recently. The manufacturing-based multinationals from the industrialized regions have served as key contributors to the export-led economic growth of many of the region's countries. Since the end of World War II, when multinationals started to rationalize their manufacturing policies worldwide on the basis of cost, Southeast Asia has served as a favorite location for their investments. Southeast Asia provided everything the multinationals wanted: attractive tax incentives on top of low tax rates, investment benefits, and cheap but trainable and increasingly educated labor offered by host countries. Consequently, multinationals poured growing investment into the region in every decade following World War II and transferred some of their manufacturing operations there.

Multinationals' managers seldom had difficulty making decisions on relocating to Southeast Asia. In many instances, host governments compiled and offered to the multinationals the information relevant to making such decisions. Because the multinationals did not design their manufacturing operations to serve local markets, they did not need local market information. To obtain production-cost advantages in their worldwide operations, the multinationals primarily needed accounting and cost data; they also required acceptable port facilities to ship the manufactured goods intended primarily for export markets. Such internal decisions to maximize operational efficiency require much less data on the local environment than a decision to serve the local market. Hence, these managers did not encounter the unavailability of information on Southeast Asian markets; or they did not consider the informational void important because rationalizing production costs surmounted in importance sales to local markets.

Southeast Asia has suffered a significant loss in foreign investment on the part of Western multinationals in the last decade as foreign companies shifted their investment to China, and more recently to India. However, this trend has slowed in the last couple of years. The Chinese inflation rate has risen significantly and investment has flowed back into several Southeast Asian countries, particularly Indonesia, Thailand, the Philippines, and Vietnam.

We finally consider the Overseas Chinese family businesses. They constitute probably the most-dominant private business grouping in Southeast Asia. As we saw in Chapter 1, the Overseas Chinese generally represent a relatively small minority among most Southeast Asian local populations; yet their economic influence in the local economy far exceeds their physical numbers. Today, they are wielding various networks to extend their reach beyond the traditional stomping grounds of Southeast Asia to many parts of the world. For example, Acer Computers holds the second-largest market share in Mexico and enjoys a competitive position in its industry in many other economically advanced developing nations. Formosa Plastics, Creative Technology, and Shangri-La Hotels are just some of the famous brand names that Overseas Chinese businessmen own. Li Ka-shing still controls Husky Oil, and following years of losses, he has moved it into a profitable situation. After losing millions learning the wireless business in Europe and selling out, Li reentered the market with the Orange network and sold it for a profit of more than US$5 billion.

STAN SHIH

Drawing Aces with Acer

STAN SHIH, FOUNDER and chairman of Acer of Taiwan, built the company from a US$25,000, 11-employee start-up to the US$14 billion company of today. Acer is the world's third-largest manufacturer of personal computers and PC parts, and one of Taiwan's few globally recognized brand names.

Shih had a humble start. He still recalls the day that his incense-maker father died and he had to help his widowed mother sell duck eggs, watermelon seeds, and lottery tickets. Acer started out in 1976 as Multitech; its main business then involved trading and consulting services for Taiwan's young information technology (IT) industry. He got into the computer industry by supplying "Made in Taiwan" computers to major PC makers around the world, but he decided that to attain viability in the future PC industry, a company had to market its own brand-name PCs. The road appeared bumpy to create and establish a brand name in an industry dominated by names such as IBM, Compaq, NEC, and Hewlett-Packard, especially for a small player such as Acer from a market unknown for high technology such as Taiwan. Shih started by achieving the number one or two market position in several rapidly developing markets (Indonesia, Malaysia, Mexico,

South Africa, and a host of other emerging markets). In 1995, the ultimate challenge of making it to the top league of PC companies in the U.S. market came true with the launch of the Aspire line of PCs. Acer introduced Aspire as a radically new-looking PC with soft shapes, cool curves, and dark, rich colors such as charcoal gray and emerald green. Aspire vaulted Acer from number nine in the U.S. market into the top five best-selling lines.

Since 1995, Acer has been making waves in various aspects of manufacturing and management practices. Analysts and researchers now regard Acer as an innovative and serious contender in IT. Shih looks at Acer as "the Dragon Dream." He said, "This dream is not mine, but is derived from a sense of the general direction and aspirations of colleagues and young people." He and his team built a business empire known as the fast-food model of PC manufacturing. Shih borrowed a concept from the fast-food industry: the company ships pre-processed ingredients to outlets to minimize preparation time, making the product just-in-time to maintain freshness and consistency. Acer manufactures components, such as caseworks, power supplies, keyboards, and monitors, at its plants in Taiwan and Malaysia and ships them to regional assembly facilities; Acer air-freights the more technology- and price-sensitive items such as motherboards, while locally procuring other components such as disk drives and memory chips. It generally keeps inventory for one week. Today, Acer forms a network of independent companies (each with substantial local shareholdings in its country) linked together to pursue Acer's Dragon Dream. Three major subgroups—Acer Group, BenQ Group, and Wistron Group—have their separate business goals.

Shih served as chairman and CEO of Acer until his retirement in late 2004, seeing Acer growing from a tiny start-up to a multibillion-dollar worldwide brand. In a June 2004 interview with CRN, Shih clarified his vision for Acer: "I would say the current Acer business vision would be my first choice. The reason is—this is the future business model: asset-light. For a knowledge-based economy, I would like an asset-light company. No factory. I don't have a lot of inventory. It means the knowledge density or content is high. A brand-name business model—an IP (intellectual property) development business model."

On his retirement from Acer, Shih established iD SoftCapital, an investment management and business consulting company, with six partners, former Acer executives, who have extensive experience in the IT industry. In 2007, Taiwan's President Chen Shui-bian appointed Shih as the special representative to the Asia-Pacific Economic Co-operation (APEC) Forum in Australia.

Historically, many Overseas Chinese—such as Singapore's Goh Cheng Liang, founder of the Wuthelam Group—started their businesses as merchants and traders. As a general rule, once the Overseas Chinese established some degree of financial stability, they would quickly move into property-related businesses and before long diversified into almost any business deemed profitable. As discussed in the previous chapter, Robert Kuok of Malaysia presents an extremely successful example of this unique diversification; his investments cover every continent save Africa and Antarctica, and his businesses range from commodities trading to beverages, utilities and infrastructural projects to hotels and resorts, media and cinema to plantations. The Overseas Chinese businesses generally displayed an intuitive, entrepreneurial, and fast decision-making style and paternalistic management. To understand how fast the Overseas Chinese act when they scent a good investment, consider Wuthelam Group's move into New Zealand property development. One of the group's most senior executives with long-time experience in the firm's property development business was visiting New Zealand and saw a property in receivership. He described his actions to us:

> An investment of 17 million Kiwi dollars may seem like a lot, but the original developers had already invested 10 million in infrastructure, had already developed one marina on the property successfully. The receiver's valuation on the land was 25 million dollars, but I had been able to bargain them down. In effect then, we would only be paying 7 million for the land itself as it had 10 million in improvements. With 7 million, I take a chance. Paying 8 million below the valuation, I also had some leeway. Based on my experience it would have been difficult to lose money on the property. Now, with greater experience and knowledge about the New Zealand market and the overall situation, we are expanding and the final investment will be over 1 billion Kiwi dollars.

GOH CHENG LIANG

Wuthelam Group: A Family Company Professionalizing

GOH CHENG LIANG was born to a poor family. In a rare interview given to the *Business Times* of Singapore (Sept. 26, 1997), he recalled, "My father was jobless. My mother was washing laundry; my sister was selling *soon kway* [a Chinese rice-noodle cake]." His first business venture, production of aerated water, ended in failure.

His first major break came in 1949 when the British army was auctioning off surplus stocks of war material. He bought several barrels of "rotten paint." He then started mixing the paint with various colors and selling it under his own brand name, Pigeon Brand Paint. As the Korean War grew in intensity, his business blossomed.

When a joint venture to distribute paint with Nippon Paint of Osaka, Sim Lim Group of Singapore, and Charoen Pokphand (CP) Group of Thailand broke up, Goh decided to continue on his own with Nippon Paint. He purchased a 60 percent interest in the resulting joint venture. Nippon Paint's expansion in Asia and its subsequent strong hold on the Asian markets is largely due to Goh's entrepreneurial drive.

He used his resulting fortune from the paint-distribution business to diversify into other areas such as property and retailing. Goh also started the Mount Elizabeth Hospital, a premier private health care center for the region, which he sold off some years ago.

Although Goh has made Nippon Paint a household name in Asia, he often attributes his success to luck. Sources close to him peg his success to his management style and his ability to judge how best to use people to obtain optimal returns from their abilities. A strong believer in his philosophy ("Have faith in your staff, they will bring in results"), he has created many millionaires among his loyal staff.

Today, the Wuthelam Group is no longer a typical paternalistically managed Chinese family company. A new influx of professional management, widely covered in the media, along with the return of his son, Goh Hup Jin, has created a new Wuthelam. With the recruitment of Koh Boon Hwee (now chairman of DBS Holdings and DBS Bank), the former managing director of Hewlett-Packard Singapore, Wuthelam began professionalizing at a rapid rate. Several Wuthelam Group companies have gone public.

Goh's genuine concern for his people is exemplified by his founding of a new company, Yenom, to house staff affected by the professionalization wave at Wuthelam. He said, "Most of the old staff cannot work with the new, very logical management; that is why I had to start this new company to house all the people who are used to the same system as me" (*Business Times*, Sept. 26, 1997). Interestingly, Yenom, the new company founded for the old staffers, has done fine—demonstrating that the old style can work well even in this modern age.

Owing to their low level of formal education, especially of business education, the founders and trusted senior executives of many Overseas Chinese businesses made decisions to invest, grow, and compete almost solely on the basis of business sense, experience, and their individual propensity to take risks. The requirements of traditional Western business information and detailed analyses of business ventures rarely occurred, if at all. The example of Wuthelam reveals every aspect of the traditional decision-making process. New Asian Emperor Robert Kuok, on whom *Forbes* bestowed the title "the World's Shrewdest Businessman," elaborated on his prejudice against hiring MBAs and using their decision-making techniques: "When I hear somebody's got an MBA, I have a feeling of dread, because normally they come to me with an over-pompous sense of their own importance. And no way are you going to prick that bubble, with the result that one day there will be a cave-in in their department. So, they learn painful lessons at my expense!" (*Forbes*, July 28, 1997, p. 94) On occasion, when truly difficult decisions had to be made, and additional information was considered necessary, the Chinese businessmen usually depended on their network of friends and well-connected government officials to supply them with the relevant information. Trust and loyalty formed central concerns; they still do. The traditional, hard data desired by Western strategic and operational planners did not appear necessary. The desired information frequently involved subjective views or beliefs that the businessmen used to increase the level of confidence in their decisions.

The second generation of more-modern Overseas Chinese executives often expresses the same doubts in the efficacy of market research as their predecessors. Stan Shih, founding chairman of Acer, a US$14 billion company, for instance, told us that he relies on "gut feel," though not on the gut feel of any specific person, not even himself. Shih believed in and relied on the collective gut feel of his team at the top of Acer. Research to him was "something which confirms the known." He argued: "You don't really need market data and information, as each decision often is not big. Although [at the founding of Acer] there was risk, the smallness of the project and the decision made the decision-making relatively easy"; and as for the use of market research, "We use it in a small way. We believe in doing things quickly. We do discuss things amongst ourselves a lot; it is like a team kind of gut feel. We implement and change things quickly. It is all implementation in the market place."

This somewhat holistic, yet intuitive, decision-making style corresponds well to an information-scarce environment and to the competitive situation in which most founders of today's great Overseas Chinese empires found themselves. As one New Asian Emperor interviewed for this book (who prefers to remain anonymous) said:

> Making decisions without feasibility studies is not a Chinese trait; it is a decision-making trait which is common to any who enter business under conditions of scarcity. If you take the risk, maybe you lose your money, but maybe you don't. If you

invest in the research or feasibility study, you don't have any
chance to win; you no longer have the money to invest.

The network system also served to effectively exclude new entrants
who lacked the Overseas Chinese business community's experience and contacts. For instance, many Southeast Asian banks have
historically had a community basis; that is, they serve particular
groups, or networks, of people, not groups of people who live within
a specific geographic area. These community bases continue today,
creating barriers to entry in some instances. As mentioned in a previous chapter, individuals who applied for business loans from banks
in Indonesia often found that all the information included in their
application had been transferred to companies (bank clients) in
the same business as the applicant, and that the related companies
had not only moved into the business but even implemented the
business plans submitted with the application (East Asia Analytical
Unit, 1995)!

Many observers have attributed the rapid growth of Overseas
Chinese family businesses in the region to their amazing speed of decision making (Chu and MacMurray, 1993); this speed and ability to
dominate access to information makes it possible to seize major business opportunities. The tremendous speed with which the Wuthelam
Group moved into New Zealand's property development indicates
just how fast the Overseas Chinese can move. As noted in previous
chapters, they are not foolhardy. As a second senior Wuthelam executive pointed out to us, the initial investment of 17 million Kiwi dollars
was only "2 to 3 percent of annual cash flow." They would have hated
to lose the money, but the company's viability would not have been
affected by losing every penny of the investment—something unlikely
to occur because the acquisition costs approximated only about two-
thirds of the property's valuation by the court receivers.

These decision-making traits add up to a different way of doing
business in Southeast and East Asia than that practiced in the
West (G. T. Haley, 1997a, 1997b; Haley and Haley, 1997, 1998,

1999; Haley & Tan, 1996; Hofstede, 1994). The differences greatly influence the Overseas Chinese networks' management and decision-making styles and practices. Researchers have posited various explanations for the differences that emerge between Asian and Western strategic decision making. For example, Haley and Tan (1996) and Haley and Haley (1997) suggested competitive advantage as a possible explanation. The Overseas Chinese networks' ability to exclude inexperienced and poorly connected competitors supports this explanation. Also, many Overseas Chinese companies have continued to employ the same holistic decision-making practices after becoming large multinationals, and long after hiring experienced, Western-trained managers away from multinational competitors—further indicating that their strategic decision-making style affords a competitive advantage. The decision-making style, and the environment in which they prosper, also weaken marketing and distribution, the primary competitive strengths for many of their multinational competitors. Western multinationals have difficulty making decisions without hard data; marketing research precedes virtually every single major competitive move. Yet in Southeast Asia, little of the desired data exists, and Asians often do not undertake or participate well in research programs. Hence, by promoting information scarcity the Overseas Chinese businessmen deny to larger, more technologically advanced Western multinationals with stronger brand names an important advantage they expect and generally have.

Hofstede (1994) argued that ethnic and cultural factors accounted for differences in decision-making styles; alternatively, Haley and Stumpf (1989) found differences in decision making traceable to personality type. Later, U.C.V. Haley (1997) detected evidence of significant personality-type differences between managerial cadres from two countries, thereby supporting Hofstede's arguments. Fei's work (1992), which traces cultural differences including perceptions and ethics to civilizational differences between the West and the East, also tends to support Hofstede's rationale.

A potent understanding of the Overseas Chinese networks' decision-making styles probably incorporates facets from all these explanations. However, Haley and Tan's categorization of Asia (1996, elaborated in the previous section) as an informational void relative to the amount of information available in industrialized economies lies unquestioned. This informational void or black hole, we have argued, has led to a unique strategic-management style for many Asian companies. Consequently, the major differences in Asian decision making stem from the information that Asian decision makers have available and desire. This information differs significantly from that used by Western managers and strategic theorists (G. T. Haley, 1997a; Haley and Tan, 1996).

For full effectiveness in Southeast Asia, Western managers need to study holistic or intuitive decision making, and to learn it fast. Social psychologists and pop gurus have studied differences between Eastern and Western thought processes, learning capabilities, and decision-making styles; yet there is little formal knowledge of Southeast Asia's holistic or intuitive decision-making styles. Haley, Haley, and Tan (2004) reported on research in cognitive psychology, but business researchers have yet to build on it. Drawing on interviews with CEOs and senior executives of the Overseas Chinese companies (some of whom we identify in the Appendix), our observations and study of Asian executives over the last 20 years (see Haley, Haley, and Tan, 2004), and our consulting and executive-development seminars, we propose several salient characteristics common to such an experience-based holistic or intuitive approach to decision making:

1. Hands-on experience
2. Transfer of knowledge
3. Qualitative information
4. Holistic information processing
5. Action-driven decision making
6. Emergent planning

Hands-on experience

To make quick decisions comfortably, without detailed analyses of hard data, managers need extensive knowledge and experience in their strategic environment. The managers must almost always approximate hands-on line managers who have experienced the company's work routines and processes, and who know firsthand the products, markets, business environment, and industry. If the managers originate from staff, without sufficient exposure to the detailed workings of the trade, they will have difficulty putting things in perspective quickly enough to make timely decisions. Consequently, and quite commonly, many senior Chinese businesspersons running huge companies remain active in all aspects of their business. Their level of involvement appears necessary for executives to comfortably make the right decisions without data support.

Kazuo Wada (1992) furnished an example where a Chinese businessman in Hong Kong responded within 15 minutes to an offer by Li Ka-shing, chairman of the Hutchinson/Cheung Kong conglomerate, to enter into a joint venture. The businessman's confidence in Li's judgment, his ability to trust Li's word, and importantly his in-depth knowledge of the business and markets under consideration allowed him to make such a rapid decision.

In our interviews with two Wuthelam Group senior executives, both recounted the story of their New Zealand property investment. The first, traditionally trained, executive pushed forward with the investment. The second was Goh Hup Jin, chairman of Nipsea Holdings, son of the founder, and a Western-trained executive, who worked in several large U.S. companies prior to joining Wuthelam Group. The Asian business press often portrays him as leading the modernization drive at Wuthelam. Goh Hup Jin's comments shed interesting light on the younger generation of management among the New Asian Emperors. First, his comments indicate a basic continuation of the traditional management style of the older generation of Overseas Chinese management, although admittedly with some modifications. Second, his comments testify to the high degree of emotional and psychic involvement that the management style entails. Goh Hup Jin told us:

> Would I have gone to New Zealand and made the same decision? No. But not because I would never decide that way; it is because I do not like the property industry. Some industries are labors of love. To make a decision in that fashion, it must be in an industry which is a labor of love. If I had gone to New Zealand and encountered a similar situation in an industry I love, yes. I would make a decision in very much the same way.

Few metaphors better convey the necessity of a hands-on, intimate knowledge of an industry than to describe work in the industry as a "labor of love."

Addressing the same subject when we interviewed him in 2007, Lippo Group's president Stephen Riady stated that most Overseas Chinese business groups were continuing to professionalize their management, but that more senior managers still like to "know the business they operate in." The present generation of Overseas Chinese CEOs generally have training in professional management techniques and have considerable experience working in Western multinationals before returning to work in the family company. They want to see all the appropriate analysis possible, but also to incorporate the information and understanding into their decision making that comes from hands-on experience.

Transfer of knowledge

Managers often find it difficult to make new decisions within new environmental contexts. However, in Southeast Asia, companies often successfully diversify into new businesses, totally different and considered noncore. This runs contrary to the conventional business wisdom of staying within one's core business and pursuing related diversification.

For an executive to function and succeed in a new industry in which he or she has no prior experience, the executive must make generalizations from past experience and transfer those generalizations into the new context. The dexterity to extract knowledge and the perspective to help one tackle new problems in different situations involves conceptualization skills different from analytical skills. Successful Southeast Asian executives have the ability to see the big picture, and to sense intuitively winners from losers. For example, in the 1960s, New Asian Emperor Li Ka-shing diversified from becoming Hong Kong's biggest plastic-flower producer to one of the most successful property developers there. A former employee recalled, "Li's great ability was to look at a building or even a site and calculate how much it was worth." Jake van der Kamp, investment strategist with HG Asia in Hong Kong, added, "He got better and better at the game" (*Asia Inc.*, Jan. 1997, p. 46). Whether or not one believes in the continuation of this characteristic decision-making style, it constitutes an accepted part of business activity in the region (Chu and MacMurray, 1993). Chu and MacMurray (1993) believe that this aspect of business in Southeast Asia must change; yet many businesspersons in the region feel it contributes importantly to their companies' growth. For example, Thailand's Charoen Pokphand Group, owned by the Chearavanont family, started in poultry farming and has since branched out into property investments and telecommunications in order to continue its rapid growth. It has done so while maintaining overall a high level of profitability, although some individual businesses seem lackluster.

A senior Overseas Chinese executive, one of the New Asian Emperors, explained the advantages of conglomerate diversification to us in this fashion:

> You put an egg in a basket; you hope it grows; it may not, it may die; then you are poor again. You go back to work, save your money and start again. I put one egg in the basket; it

grew and I had some money so I put another. I found that the more different eggs I put in the basket, the more opportunities I had to put more eggs in. Diversification brings opportunity, and opportunity brings growth.

Qualitative information

Southeast Asian executives appear to take unnecessary risks by not undertaking sufficient research or analysis before acting; however this appearance may prove misleading. The executives often process myriad bits of information and consider several alternatives in depth before they take action. They differ from their Western counterparts in that for the Southeast Asian executives, the process may occur almost completely internally. Although their decision making may involve a high degree of articulation, the Southeast Asian executives may not present the results in detailed, written, analytical forms. Lippo's Stephen Riady told us that executives who made decisions based exclusively on the techniques of professional management were making "riskier decisions" than most senior Overseas Chinese executives liked to make.

When we asked Wee Ee Cheong, deputy president (now CEO) of the United Overseas Bank Group, how he goes about making his decisions, he responded that he:

> doesn't let figures influence his decisions. [He] looks at the business first, sizes up the staff [his bank's staff] who wrote the business report, how thorough they were in their research, what assumptions they made in arriving at their conclusion.

> [He] often looks at the business, the management; who is in charge [he likes to talk to people at all levels in the organization; often middle level people give him the best information for his decision]; the qualitative aspects of the decision. Numbers often come last. They are used to confirm the decision rather than to arrive at the decision.

Interestingly, Wee Ee Cheong is one of the second generation of Overseas Chinese managers, not a member of the founding genera-tion. His father, chairman and former CEO of the United Overseas Bank Group, Wee Cho Yaw, with whom we also discussed strategic-management approaches, takes an even more qualitative approach in his decision making.

Overseas Chinese executives almost always use external sources of information when making strategic decisions. Our experience indicates that executives will actively seek out information and search for the critical pieces that have an impact on their final deci-sion. Riady, who has a degree in business, has emphasized to us that analysis is not enough. He stated, "If you are risk averse, you have to analyze an investment, you have to visit the investment, you have to be visible if you want to understand it. Analysis is not enough." However, executives are less likely to refer to documented evidence or data in published form. They prefer to use sources of often quali-tative, even subjective information, such as friends, business associ-ates, government officials, and other people whose judgment they trust, and in whom they personally trust. They strive for on-site visi-bility, meeting face-to-face with people, and understanding how they have come to hold the opinions they have. They may often travel to the local scene to check personally on the reliability of local infor-mation, rather than rely on secondary information. Their contacts and connections among local sources often consist of people who can supply up-to-date, accurate information that may not be pub-lished. Such firsthand information from original sources may prove superior to any other available alternatives. Consequently, with hindsight, many of the decisions that the Southeast Asian execu-tives make appear correct.

Network building goes beyond linking oneself to some sen-ior government official or great industrialist. Southeast Asian businessmen, though criticized for not building their internal bases of managerial talent, often seek out promising individuals who they feel will prove valuable contacts in the future.

Holistic information processing

Conventional analytical problem solving, as taught in business schools and universities, tends to stress a sequential, systematic, and step-by-step approach to solving problems and making decisions. This approach proves most effective when, at each step, managers can obtain the proper inputs for use. The approach may prove optimal in a situation where managers can readily generate or purchase needed data. In an informational void situation, though, managers may find the approach unworkable.

Wee Cho Yaw articulated to us that there may be some generational differences among the New Asian Emperors' strategic decision-making styles. Before, with limited data, the information did exist in different forms. However, he said of the managers of his generation:

> We talk breakfast, lunch, and attend social functions to exchange views and ideas; market information is often exchanged in social settings. Business decisions are made after factoring in all these views and input. However, to a large extent, decisions are made on gut feel and business acumen.

The experience-based intuitive model described here views the problem in totality; managers take general approaches to problems, define parameters intuitively, and explore solutions holistically. Such intuitive models appear to resemble Asian thinking and learning processes. They form alternative modes of decision making that work well in many situations, especially in those environments in which they have evolved.

Action-driven decision making

Speed constitutes one key characteristic of decision making in the Southeast Asian business context. Executives often make key decisions without consulting anyone. Their preference appears to be for action. Numerous stories exist of well-known Southeast Asian executives who decided on important matters in minutes and implemented the results almost immediately. The quickness also reflects the empowerment and accountability of the executives' actions. Executives often have great latitude in deciding matters. Long debates and committee meetings rarely occur.

The Overseas Chinese decision-making model does reflect an authoritative management style. However, when one person has responsibility in a situation, and the authority to make final judgment, a little authoritativeness can move things more quickly, get work done faster, and allow adroit exploitation of opportunities. Tan Kah Kee, one of the giants of the Overseas Chinese community in the 20th century, took an initial early gamble; he made the decision to buy 500 acres of uncleared jungle to plant with pineapples to supply his pineapple-canning factory. Once he cleared the land, he decided to bet on future opportunities rather on his past successes. Rather than planting pineapples, he planted rubber trees. He had to move fast to take advantage of all the new opportunities for rubber; the year was 1905, and as Tan Kah Kee saw automobiles assuming importance, he had no time to waste (Yong, 1987).

Emergent planning

The Chinese networks engage in what Henry Mintzberg termed emergent planning (Mintzberg, 1987, 1994; Mintzberg and Waters, 1985). Strategies bubble up through individual companies and also collectively through the networks. Typically, news, rumors, or insider information reaches the networks' managers and creates interest. The managers then seek confirming evidence, gauge available resources, and make and implement decisions. As further information becomes available, the managers modify strategies. Strategies emerge from the managers' and the companies' learned business behaviors. When

CEO Victor Fung described to us the expansion of Li & Fung, he could have been paraphrasing Mintzberg's description of emergent planning. He said that the changes he and his brother, William, instituted "definitely evolved. We saw ourselves as a regional player that was China-centric. But after we acquired Inchcape Buying Services, it expanded our horizons and we saw that we could source from India. We started changing; as the manufacturing environment evolved and became global, we began to view ourselves as a global sourcing agent." Thus, the strategy emerged from the confluence of the emerging manufacturing environment with the capabilities and input bubbling up from Inchcape's managers.

Steven Chan, who was executive chairman when we first spoke, of Superior Multi-Packaging Ltd. Singapore, a company owned by the Goh family, explained the company's planning processes to us: "We've got a five-year plan that we revise every year. All our people involved in our China operations will have some ideas. They will have ideas of why we did not achieve the growth we want in China; they will have ideas of how to achieve 20 percent growth in China, and we revise our plans accordingly." This bubbling-up process takes advantage of line managers' experiences and knowledge, and the strategies developed to deal with the changing business environment. Line managers often lack training in planning technologies; but their experiences and abilities to process information holistically, and incorporate those experiences into an in-depth understanding of business situations, often helps them outperform staff analysts at headquarters, and it always helps them arrive at their proposed solution faster than headquarters can. Chan identified one line manager who Superior Multi-Packaging values and who showed significant managerial potential as a "midlevel engineer." The manager appeared highly intelligent and well trained, but not in traditional business techniques and terminologies. Without Superior Multi-Packaging's proactive efforts to acquire and understand his strategic suggestions, the company would have lost his contributions.

Chinese companies also display emergent planning in searching for local joint venture (JV) partners. Partnership possibilities emerge, preferably within the originating partners' business networks. The potential partners' decision to join together hinges largely on their confidence in the proposing managers' judgment and abilities. The managers' suggested strategies bubble up within their companies, through their top management, seeping through their JV partners and permeating through the entire business network. In effect, Chinese companies have enlarged Henry Mintzberg's emergent planning beyond individual company boundaries to include associated groups of companies.

The network-management system of the Overseas Chinese enjoys several unique characteristics; yet as the Wuthelam Group's senior executives indicated to us, strategic factors of import in other parts of the world, such as resource scarcity, also influence the Overseas Chinese strategic decisions. Given these observations from the New Asian Emperors, one can more fully comprehend their strengths and weaknesses through a strategic-planning model that classifies their strategic processes. In our next chapter, we present a conceptualization of strategic planning developed in the West that helps us better understand the New Asian Emperor's strategic decisions and managing for competitive advantage in Asia generally. In the final chapter of this book, we present such a strategic-planning model.

CHAPTER 5

Strategic Management of the Overseas Chinese Business Groups: Deciphering Patterns

> What belonged to our family 100 years ago still belongs to us. It is our culture not to risk what great-grandfather built.
>
> —**Vuttichai Wanglee,** referring to his great grandfather, Ian Siew-Wang, first of the great founding fathers to defeat the third-generation curse of Chinese fortunes

In the 1990s, researchers and the media granted a great deal of coverage to Overseas Chinese companies and their management. In the wake of the Asian financial crisis and of SARS, attention returned to the region's Overseas Chinese business groups. Yet few made a concerted effort to understand the strategic implications of their management style, and even fewer studied how this style evolved. Most either tried to describe the decision-making processes, explain the various consequences of these styles, or extrapolate on their origins and significance; but few placed the Overseas Chinese networks' strategic decision-making style within knowledge management or strategic-planning theoretical constructs. Many still argue that the Overseas Chinese do not conduct strategic planning.

In this chapter, we place the Overseas Chinese strategic-management style within established knowledge-management and strategic-planning constructs. By doing so, we enhance understanding of the Overseas Chinese networks' strategic capabilities, strengths, and weaknesses. By reinterpreting their behavior through familiar lenses, we heighten our ability to predict the actions of the Overseas Chinese and can better understand the changes occurring in their management. Those who study behavioral implications will have the tools to judge the "uprightness" of the Overseas Chinese managers they encounter. We note here that the Confucian influences on management that we have identified influence virtually all Southeast and East Asian cultures, but in varying degrees; although the Overseas Chinese dominate business operations in the region, not all Southeast Asian managers are Overseas Chinese.

First, we review some major theoretical knowledge-management and strategic-planning constructs. We then incorporate the Overseas Chinese managers' traditional decision processes within these constructs. Next, we describe how the Overseas Chinese craft strategies and use their core competencies to gain competitive advantage in their business environment. This description should enable companies and executives that compete against, or cooperate with, the Overseas Chinese to understand and judge their behavior (as well as their own) in context.

Tacit Knowledge and the Informational Black Hole

As described in the previous chapter, our extensive interviews with several hundred CEOs and senior executives of Overseas Chinese companies (some of whom we mention in the Appendix), and our in-depth observation of their strategic management styles, confirm that these executives emphasize action over cognition, tacit knowledge over explicit knowledge, human judgment over mechanistic information processing, and ends over means. Michael Polanyi's theories and themes clarified our understanding of these characteristics. Polanyi studied skillful performance, which he insisted involved the whole person and resulted from tacit knowing. Whereas Western philosophy since the Enlightenment has focused primarily on clarifying reasoning, Polanyi studied human action and pragmatism. His discussions encompassed knowledge, which people possess, and knowing, which people demonstrate in action (see Nissen, 2006). We argue that the strategic management styles of the Overseas Chinese demonstrate tacit knowing.

Polanyi's contribution of "tacit knowledge" (1962, 1966) has influenced theories of routine, practice, and knowledge management in organizations. It explains to some extent how Overseas Chinese managers engage in creative problem solving through problem specification, generation of alternatives, and evaluation of those alternatives. For Polanyi, *tacit* referred to the unarticulated elements of human knowledge. According to Polanyi, tacit knowing implied mind-body holism, and this fusion resulted in skillful performance. Skillful performance in strategizing (or any other endeavor) included activity, aspects of which managers must learn through practice and which neither managers nor analysts can capture fully in written or verbal instructions. Overseas Chinese management appears to rely to a higher degree on tacit knowledge than does Western management, which draws more on codified or explicit management. Nonaka and Takeuchi (1995) used the term *internalization* to refer to conversion of explicit knowledge to tacit knowledge. This internalization, they argued, forms an essential component of developing expertise. Tacit knowledge therefore includes knowledge of which the Overseas Chinese managers have awareness, but which they cannot articulate in rules and procedures. Indeed, Polanyi suggested that tacit knowledge should remain unarticulated and subsidiary (that is, nonlocal) if one is to perform skillfully.

As the Overseas Chinese managers attend focally to a specific problem or activity, other aspects of knowing become subsidiary (see Polanyi 1962). Indeed, many have indicated to us that when they made what eventually turned out to be optimal decisions, they operated in "the zone" and at peak performance. The managers attended to the objects of their focal awareness from a set of tools and background knowledge. As Polanyi (1962) predicted, the managers became distracted and their performance flagged if they shifted their attention from focal tasks to subsidiary knowledge that they brought to the task. The previous chapter described how managers often ceased to attend focally to codified or explicit knowledge as they became more skilled practitioners. Intellectual passion and creativity motivated them to pursue more problems and tackle them, and these pursuits in turn reflected their personal values and visions of reality. The managers also told us that they often see strategic solutions in prior, seemingly unrelated problems. As Polanyi described, they saw symbolic representations of their problems and drew on prior knowledge as critical to the search for solutions. They used inherently personal criteria to identify and test patterns across industries and sectors, and to generate strategic solutions.

In the first section of this book, we covered the Overseas Chinese managers' cultural and societal roots. Polanyi also analyzed how rationality and knowledge emerge within communities and how cultural heritage infuses knowledge: "Human thought grows only within language, and since language can exist only in a society, all thought is rooted in society" (Polanyi, 1959, p. 60). By participating in a community, the Overseas Chinese come to share a set of commitments that shape their identity, rationality, and knowledge. These commitments influence their faculty to interpret patterns, language, and symbols, and their ability to grasp part-whole relationships, which in turn contribute to their ability to generate creative solutions for problems (Polanyi, 1969).

In the previous chapter, we elaborated on the strategic business environment, including the informational black hole and relations with governments, which allows Overseas Chinese to excel in acquiring relevant information to enhance their strategic performance and competitiveness. Polanyi's theories (and others' such as Foucault, 1980) shed more light on this reciprocal relationship between knowledge and power: knowledge confers power, and power shapes acquisition and evolution of knowledge. Powerful actors within companies and societies, such as the Overseas Chinese senior executives and Southeast Asian government officials, influence knowledge acquisition not only through allocating resources but also through granting access to knowledge and conferring legitimacy on it. Next, we elaborate on how tacit knowledge shows itself in Overseas Chinese strategic planning and why most researchers ignore it.

Strategic Planning and the Networks

Unlike the Asian strategic environment and management style we elaborated in the previous chapter, a determining factor in Western management involves the virtually unlimited wealth of codified information available to anyone with the desire and wit to find and use it. Table 5.1 (G. T. Haley, 1997a) summarizes two of the dominant characteristics of strategic-planning processes propounded by prominent theorists that assume importance in our discussion of Overseas Chinese strategic planning. Most established understandings of strategic planning incorporate (1) abundance and ready availability of data on company industries, markets, and environments; and (2) significant investment in staff to collect, collate, and analyze the data. Staff then interpret the information generated and develop strategic recommendations for senior management.

TABLE 5.1: *Characteristics of Strategic-Planning Processes*

Strategic Theorists	Staff/Line Dependent	Data/Experience Dependent
Hofer and Schendel	Staff	Data
Porter	Staff	Data
Prahalad and Hamel	Staff/line	Data/experience
Mintzberg	Staff/line	Data/experience

Planning, classically

Charles Hofer and Dan Schendel (1978) were among the earliest conceptualizers of a classic strategic-planning process. Michael Porter also used many of the same building blocks for planning; hence, they share characteristics. First, their processes depend on the ability to acquire a large amount of relatively high-quality internal and external information. Also, their processes need a wealth of data because the planning demands analytical and procedural rationality. To employ a system of analytical rationality requires largely sequential collection, analysis, and interpretation of data to generate the desired information. More high-quality data fed into analytical schemes should, in these theories, generate increasingly higher-quality analysis, thereby aiding managers to achieve better decisions.

Managers collect, analyze, and interpret the data within fixed, perceptual constructs of the relationships between the company and the environment. These perceptual constructs collectively form underlying theories of how the world works—and should work—with respect to the managers' particular problems. By emphasizing threats and opportunities in the external environment and the company's own strengths and weaknesses, classical planning processes assume that managers can measure and understand the relationships between their company and the environment through collecting and analyzing data within a positivist framework. Several problems may confound these classical-planning processes.

First, if the managers' perceptual constructs (their underlying theories of all the variables involved, and their influences and interactions) have validity, then the strategic plans may achieve success—but there are no guarantees. For effective planning, managers should use data that also reliably represent their strategies. If significant errors surround understanding or measurement of important variables, managers are unlikely to plan for effective strategies.

Second, the processes depend largely on the company's possessing substantial staff to collect, collate, and analyze large amounts of data to understand the business environment and decision situation, and then to generate recommendations for strategic action. Frequently, company staff have little or no line-management or operational experience. Their understanding of business situations often revolves around their familiarity with analytical techniques, and collection and interpretation of data; they have little knowledge of the nuances of business operations, relationships with stakeholders, or any direct familiarity and understanding of the markets of the business. These strategic planning processes, which so many Western managers learn in the world's premier MBA programs, separate the company's minds and hands (Mintzberg, 1987, 1994); usually, they have no place for the "hearts" or "guts" with which many of the New Asian Emperors (as we elaborated in the previous chapter) sense their strategic opportunities.

Henry Mintzberg (1987, 1994) distinguished between two kinds of strategic planning that involve the activities of both the hands and the mind. Classic strategic planning processes and concepts represent the mind's activities in planning because of their heavy dependence on staff and data. They require substantial investment in data acquisition, intense mining of those data for information, and developing plans based on interpretation of the information generated. However, planning of the mind does not require line-management experience, familiarity with problems associated with managing a production line or sales force, direct knowledge and experience in dealing with the company's market, or direct interaction with the customers or suppliers to understand their problems and manner of thinking. In fact, planning of the mind requires no direct responsibility for generating corporate profits. The staff analysts may have purely academic understanding of their business, market, and environment; their expertise lies in the analytical tools they employ, not in their experiential understanding of the business.

Developing core competencies

C. K. Prahalad and Gary Hamel are probably the most influential strategic-planning theorists of their time. In their seminal 1990 article, they argued for a more internal focus to strategic planning. They contended that the most successful planning efforts of a business occur when strategies exploit core competencies, or key skills, refined and honed over the years in various business activities. Prahalad and Hamel indicated that, by design or by coincidence, successful companies develop a collection of skills at which they excel, and which constitute the basis for their success. These key skills they termed the company's core competencies.

In any industry or market, more than one set of skills can contribute to core competency; hence, companies in the same industry and serving the same market can possess different core competencies. The relative competitive advantages of core competencies change over time because of various factors such as industrial, technological, and product life cycle or basic and applied innovations in the industry. For skills to contribute to a company's core competencies, they must:

1. Offer potential access to various markets
2. Make important contributions to the perceived benefits companies deliver to their customers
3. Be difficult to imitate

Unlike Hofer and Schendel, and Porter, Prahalad and Hamel make no pronouncements about how to plan. Strategic planning drawing on core competencies may or may not depend on a substantial investment in obtaining a great deal of high-quality information or a huge staff. The Overseas Chinese companies obviously appear to wield their skills to enhance their core competencies; Mintzberg's concept of crafting strategy sheds more light on these strategic behaviors.

Crafting strategies

Mintzberg (1987, 1994) and Mintzberg and Waters (1985) have championed another approach to strategic planning that draws on the crafting of strategies.

Using the metaphor of a craftsman making pottery, Mintzberg (1987) described strategic planning as involving both the mind and hands. The mind's activity stresses classical, strategic-planning activities such as SWOT analysis and value chain analysis. He (Mintzberg, 1987) also argued that strategic planning remains incomplete if it excludes either the mind's or the hands' activity. He postulated that strategic planning consists of minds and hands performing four activities:

1. Detecting discontinuity
2. Knowing the business
3. Managing patterns
4. Reconciling change and continuity

Detecting discontinuity

Mintzberg argued that a company earns profits primarily during periods of stability; hence, management's major job involves detecting discontinuity as early as possible and adapting their strategies to meet it most successfully. If minor discontinuities occur, managers should make minimal changes to an historically successful strategy and minimize disruption to the company's smooth functioning. If major discontinuities occur, managers should decide on the best strategies to move quickly from discontinuity to stability to maximize profits once again.

Knowing the business

Mintzberg contended that the best planning and implementation of plans occurs when management knows the business of its company inside and out. This stipulation holds especially true for the hands' activities in strategic planning. Hands' knowledge arises through day-to-day responsibility for line activities. Through managing line activities, managers learn the nuances, potential problems, and synergies that can arise as functions of the company conduct business and interact.

Managing patterns

Mintzberg indicated that managers can most efficiently and profitably manage periods of stability by developing and recognizing patterns. In particular, managers must recognize the patterns that emerge in their company's environments and business activities. Additionally, managers must develop behavioral patterns to manipulate efficiently the controllable variables and influence effectively the environmental patterns. In effect, managers must manage the relevant patterns so that they interact and mesh together optimally.

Reconciling change and continuity

According to Mintzberg, a manager's primary function involves reconciling changes and continuities. In uncertain times, managers should not manage change, but rather work through the discontinuity as quickly as possible to reestablish stability. During periods of change, profits appear uncertain and highly variable, making the transition to a period of stability desirable where profits assume more certainty.

Earlier in the section, we described Mintzberg's concept of planning with the mind. Mintzberg developed his alternate concept of planning with hands by observing his wife, a professional potter, make her pottery. She planned with the mind, selecting the correct amount and type of clay for her pottery and producing that on her pottery wheel. He noted that the resultant figure was sometimes not one she had planned. While working, she often found that miscalculations, fresh insights, whims, or instincts influenced her to produce something different for her market. She operated instinctively so that her ability to innovate appeared to draw on her profound, ingrained knowledge of the craft and market. The resulting product incorporated her strategy. She generated her strategy purposefully, or in reaction to unexpected developments, but she could do so intuitively only because of a profound knowledge of her craft, business, and market. Acquiring astute knowledge through experience in making and selling her product, she basically embodied line-management experience and tacit knowledge of her profession.

Line management's knowledge and experience are significantly different from that of staff. Line management and personnel acquire all the necessary components and raw materials to produce the products; they deal with the nuances of translating R&D prototypes for the production line; they work to manufacture their products in the most efficient way possible given the specific capital equipment and personnel the company possesses; they develop the logistical and distribution channels that move the products to market; and finally, they interact daily with customers and their problems. By facing and dealing with routine problems, line management and personnel develop instinctive understanding of the requirements for success in their industry and market; their unique understanding for success often has richer and more textured tones than those that staff personnel develop through their analyses.

Mintzberg (1987, and Mintzberg and Waters, 1985) also categorized strategic plans as directed or emergent. Directed strategic plans develop through the classical strategic planning processes discussed earlier in this section. Emergent strategic plans evolve from the collective, behavioral patterns of employees (Mintzberg, 1987, 1994; Mintzberg and Waters, 1985) as they react to environmental stimuli. When crafting strategy, they argue, for the best planning, managers need both directed and emergent strategic planning.

Emergent strategic plans develop through the management groups' collective experience and the company's learned business behaviors. Mintzberg described the process as a "bubbling up" of strategic plans from the lower levels of management to higher levels; line managers react to problems they face in their business activities, which the company's official strategic or operational plans either ignore or cannot solve.

Mintzberg also noted that strategic planning through a bubbling-up process can have competitive dimensions. As personnel probably encounter the same problems or similar ones, the individuals probably develop a range of solutions from slight variations on the same theme to entirely different solutions for solving an immediate problem. If the company faces minor discontinuities, these local adaptations generally maintain the company's profitability without senior managers' attention. However, if the company faces a major discontinuity, the local adaptations bubble upward toward senior managers; the adaptations compete for senior managers' attention to be incorporated into, or to form the basis of, the company's new primary strategic postures—their attempts to reattain stability.

We believe that Mintzberg's conceptualization of crafting strategy best describes and explains the strategic management of the Overseas Chinese and their reliance on tacit knowledge for excellent performance. In the following sections of the chapter, we demonstrate the similarities between Mintzberg's concepts and the traditional management practices of the Overseas Chinese.

A Summary of Overseas Chinese Management Practices

We present here a short summary of the Overseas Chinese management practices delineated in detail in the previous chapters. The Overseas Chinese strategic-planning methods emphasize line management through depending on soft data and on intimate, intuitive understanding of the business and the environment. As Haley and Tan described (1996), their managers disdain separation of planning and doing and emphasize action. These tendencies allow Overseas Chinese companies to employ and use fewer staff people than Western companies do. For example, the average size of Hong Kong companies shrank by 59 percent from 1954 to 1984, although their operations expanded significantly during this period (Redding, 1986).

Haley and Tan (1996) also noted five practices of Overseas Chinese management, and Haley and Haley (1998) added a sixth. These characteristics are:

1. Hands-on experience
2. Transfer of knowledge across businesses
3. Qualitative information
4. Holistic information processing
5. Action-driven decision making
6. Emergent planning

Enormous similarities in virtually every aspect of strategic planning appear when we compare the management practices of the Overseas Chinese with the conceptualization of strategic planning developed by Mintzberg and his colleagues; in the next section, we elaborate on these similarities for a fresh understanding of the New Asian Emperors' strategic behaviors.

The Overseas Chinese and crafting strategy

In his theoretical constructs, Mintzberg captures many facets of the Overseas Chinese networks' strategic-planning processes and modes (G. T. Haley, 1997a). He observed that the best strategic plans incorporate directed and emergent elements, and that strategic plans often evolve from the collective, behavioral patterns of employees (Mintzberg, 1987, 1994; Mintzberg and Waters, 1985) as they react to environmental stimuli. This observation is an apt description of the New Asian Emperors' strategic-planning processes.

Because of their founders' characteristics, emergent strategic planning appears prevalent among the Overseas Chinese companies. Haley and Tan (1996) described how the founders of most of the Overseas Chinese companies, though highly intelligent, had little formal education and even less management education. Hence, their decision making evolved within a different perspective of what constitutes acceptable data from what most Western managers have; Overseas Chinese managers used data drawn from their experience, advice from trusted friends, and their perception of the situation.

With soft data, strategy emerges from the Overseas Chinese managers' interaction with their environment. A good example occurred when a senior executive in the Wuthelam Group saw a property development in receivership and immediately reacted on the basis of his knowledge of and experience in the industry. For the typical Overseas Chinese company, news, rumors, or insider information reaches an executive and creates interest. The executive then seeks out confirming evidence and gauges available resources. The executive analyzes the situation, and makes and implements decisions. As the implementation proceeds, further information becomes available, and the executive's strategy emerges and is fleshed out; he or she stands firm, continues along the same path, or makes the strategic alterations deemed necessary. The strategies the company follows emerge from the executive's and the company's learned business behaviors and their increasing collection of knowledge dealing with the specific situation of the company's investment.

If the executives feel the need for a strategic partner, the company seeks one out. Though major Overseas Chinese companies have family bases, and major individual companies form significant conglomerates, potential partners within the Overseas Chinese networks base their decisions largely on the confidence and trust they have in the proposing executives' judgment and managerial ability. When the strategy moves from one for a single company to one adopted by the company's network of associates, it resembles Mintzberg's bubbling-up process of strategy development. Although this bubbling-up process usually occurs on an intracompany basis, within the Overseas Chinese networks, it regularly occurs on a supracompany basis.

How the Overseas Chinese plan

Detecting discontinuity and qualitative data

Mintzberg specified detecting discontinuity as the essence of strategic planning; Haley and Tan (1996) discerned this process when analyzing how Overseas Chinese managers use contacts within local governments and communities as primary sources of data. Through their web of associates, the Overseas Chinese managers determine potential changes in government policy or in the business, social, and economic environment that can cause discontinuities and force divestment or a change of business strategy. United Overseas Bank's Chairman Wee Cho Yaw alluded to detecting discontinuity when he told us, "Market information is often exchanged in social settings." Managers discussed and analyzed information in these social gatherings to determine the state of affairs and ascertain if any changes would affect their business. The Overseas Chinese businessmen's trust in each other evolved over years of friendship and business dealings; Chinese businessmen and their associates formed a network among themselves for gathering and disseminating information.

Knowing the business and hands-on experience

Knowing the business constitutes another of Mintzberg's characteristics and translates directly into the hands-on experience identified by Haley and Tan (1996). Mintzberg emphasized that managers must have an intimate knowledge of their business—its markets, products, distribution and logistical systems, production processes, and operations. Line management experience offers an excellent avenue to garner such intimate knowledge. Overseas Chinese managers emphasize active, intimate participation in all important aspects of their companies' activities, products and markets. They also stress getting one's hands dirty in company operations, and the need to deal with more than descriptive statistics. A quote from a Singaporean entrepreneur, Aw Kim Chen, speaking about the

WEE CHO YAW

United Overseas Bank: Growing Steadily

WEE CHO YAW, THE CHAIRMAN of United Overseas Bank Group (UOB), is a second-generation banker who took over his father's bank and expanded it into one of Singapore's biggest, alongside Overseas Chinese Banking Corporation and the Development Bank of Singapore. The Asian financial crisis did not affect family ownership of the business group significantly; it fell from 30.85 percent in 1996 to 26.05 percent in 2002.

Over the years, Wee actively pursued a policy of acquisition, diversification, and international expansion. Today, the Wee family's interests extend beyond banking and financial services; they also have interests in property development, hotel management, trading, manufacturing, and the travel industry in many parts of the world.

UOB's status as a leading bank in the region is partly due to an innovative and aggressive marketing and expansion strategy, and partly to a series of acquisitions. In 1971, it took over Chung Khiaw Bank, then in succession through 1987 Lee Wah Bank, Far Eastern Bank, and Industrial Commercial Bank. With the banking market saturated in Singapore, UOB has plans to push its operations further into the region. Wee said, "The banks can't grow very much in Singapore. We have to move out and go regional, perhaps even global."

Wee is confident about China, saying, "We speak the same language. Some 70 percent of Singapore's population is Chinese, and virtually all the first generation hail from China. There are still a lot of connections." With personal contacts, confidence, and trust, UOB has responded to the Singaporean government's investment in China by opening up offices there. Wee looks at China as a medium- to long-term investment situation.

As the old Chinese saying goes, "Fortune does not last three generations." However, the Wee family fortune has grown from a small bank to a large, diversified group. The third generation has reached the stature of senior management and shows no sign of diminishing anytime soon. Together with a solid team of high-caliber professional managers, many recruited from top international banks, the third generation, represented by Wee's son, Wee Ee Cheong, has taken charge of operations.

Like all truly successful Chinese businessmen, Wee Cho Yaw is a prominent Chinese leader in his home country, Singapore. He is involved in several civic organizations, and is on the board of many other business and social organizations. As the honorary president of the Singapore Chamber of Commerce and Industry and president of the Singapore Hokkien Huay Kuan, Wee plays the role of a Chinese community elder. Today, the day-to-day running of his business is being passed over to the third generation. As Wee Ee Cheong said, "The key job is to spot talents and bring them into the bank."

startup of his rubber manufacturing business, indicates this characteristic clearly (Chan and Chiang, 1994):

> I alone transacted business with the foreign countries. I also dealt with the local businessmen. I did the purchasing myself. I also took charge of the technical aspects of the factory, putting to use the rubber processing techniques which I had learnt when I was working in the Lam Aik Rubber Factory.

As the quote reveals, Aw Kim Chen was intrinsically involved in every aspect of his business. His experiences gave him the intimate, intuitive knowledge of his business that forms the keystone to the intuitive decision making and tacit knowledge that distinguish the Overseas Chinese. Also, only small companies allow such intrinsic, intimate involvement in all aspects of their business; this is a factor that the Overseas Chinese recognize in their organizational structures. Most Overseas Chinese businesses remain relatively small; over time, the total size of all of a family's businesses may add up to a large conglomerate. Additionally, when Overseas Chinese companies grow beyond any individual's abilities to undertake all of Aw's activities, employees' duties change; owners concentrate on managerial, financial, and investment decisions, and trusted subordinates on the production floor concentrate on manufacturing, purchasing, and sales.

LI & FUNG

Traders Extraordinaire

MOST OVERSEAS CHINESE companies started as trading companies. As they grew, they diversified into other businesses; many moved away from trading. Over the last two decades, the trading business has

---

become one of the most difficult and competitive industries in Asia. Even the old, huge traditional European trading companies such as Inchcape and East Asiatic have suffered. Few have been able to develop value-added activities that would justify their existence. Li & Fung is the exception. Not only has it survived, it has been able to supply value-added services to its associates in the distribution channel. The company has differentiated by piecing together and managing value chains in companies across the industrialized countries. Indeed, today Li & Fung is the world's largest contract supply-chain management firm. The company manages front-end design, marketing, and sales in Hong Kong, and production in a range of developing countries, including Bangladesh, Thailand, and China. Chances are Li & Fung touched some piece of clothing you are wearing (Haley, Haley, and Tan, 2004).

Li & Fung was founded about 90 years ago by the grandfather of its present chairman, Victor Fung. Hong Kong's boom days of the 1960s and 1970s, created by its low-cost manufacturing base, also benefited the company. Rapidly increasing exports and the constant need for brokering between U.S. buyers and Hong Kong manufacturers created a prosperous niche for Li & Fung. In 1973, the company went public, and in 1995, made headlines in purchasing Inchcape Buying Service (IBS), a major rival from parent company Inchcape, a British conglomerate. Victor Fung said: "A product costs US$1.00 when it comes out of the factory in Asia. By the time it gets to the retail shelves in the U.S. it is going to cost US$4.00. The secret is to try to earn a bigger share of that 4:1 mark-up."

Fung holds a Ph.D. in business economics from Harvard University. He serves as the highly visible chairman of one of Hong Kong's most prominent agencies, the Hong Kong Trade Development Council, and has won wide acclaim for both his business acumen and his public service to Hong Kong. He and brother William have worked hard to move Li & Fung up the value chain at a time when profit margins were being squeezed and most trading companies were having trouble just surviving. The growing sophistication of buyers and sellers alike threatens to eliminate trading houses as intermediary altogether. Rather than fleeing the industry, Li & Fung has responded by serving both their upstream and downstream customers. They have become involved in their customers' design, marketing, and planning products at one end and in the packaging, shipping, and distribution of those products at the other end. The company tailors its services to clients, sourcing products globally for Western retailers that simply wish to offer the brands or extending services by even managing the client's brand, as it does for Levi Strauss in Asia.

Li & Fung has survived and prospered by seeing opportunities and value where others did not, and integrating modern business concepts into an ancient business.

Managing patterns and holistic information processing

Mintzberg argued that primary duties of business strategists include perceiving and managing the emerging patterns of company operations and markets. Haley and Tan (1996) similarly identified managing patterns in the holistic information processing of the Overseas Chinese. In both instances, the strategists rely on perceptions, not on hard data or on collective manifestations of it that could display significant distortion. These perceptions of holistic data, viewed as patterns, lead the strategists to infer the company's present and future relationships with its internal and external environments; the perceptions also present avenues to manage company resources effectively and optimize present and future benefits. Overseas Chinese managers use networks to obtain the necessary perceptions about their business, the market environment, and coming changes; these views collectively form the patterns that they manage.

Haley and Tan (1996) also detected how the Overseas Chinese manage patterns in the transfer of knowledge. They identified how Overseas Chinese managers extrapolate what they have learned and experienced in one product or market to another unrelated product or market. By considering similarities and dissimilarities of the products and markets, the managers are also considering similarities and dissimilarities in the patterns of behavior and requirements for success in both venues. These similarities are the factors that help turn a "different egg" into a "new opportunity," as the long-time, senior executive from Wuthelam Group described it to us.

Reconciling change and continuity and the networks

Mintzberg argued that in order to optimize a company's performance, a strategist must encourage the emergence of some patterns, and delay or even prevent the emergence of others, thereby reconciling change and continuity. Through their web of associates, most especially local-government associates, the Overseas Chinese managers seek information—and where possible, they also pursue business opportunities and lobby for or against promulgation of laws, regulations, and privileged positions within desired markets and industries. In this fashion, Overseas Chinese managers strive to enhance patterns of change and continuity that enhance their strengths and minimize their weaknesses.

The Overseas Chinese have proven enormously successful in their lobbying efforts, often building monopolies in strategic Southeast Asian industries through key contacts and connections. Robert Kuok has had great success in this arena. In 1959, he founded Malaysian Sugar Manufacturing. At the time, Malaysia had no sugar plantations, but Kuok planted 2,600 hectares in a partnership with the government's Federal Land Development Authority. Thus, Kuok secured a near-monopoly of Malaysia's sugar market. In 1964, he opened his first sugar refinery. When he moved to Indonesia in the mid-1970s, he achieved dominance of the Indonesian sugar market through similar means. Kuok's long-term investments in Malaysia and other Southeast Asian countries secured his reputation. Governments in the region learned that they could trust him to work for national as well as personal advantage. An executive with Kuok's flagship Malaysian company, Perlis Plantations, succinctly explained Kuok's special relations with the Malaysian government: "We did our national service." We note here that many in the West disparagingly refer to this system as crony capitalism (see, for example, Studwell, 2007); yet, it prevails across Asia and contributes to the Overseas Chinese managers' tacit knowledge and strategic expertise. The next section explores how their managers' tacit knowledge translates into the Overseas Chinese companies' core competencies.

The Overseas Chinese and their core competencies

The Overseas Chinese have tended to follow conglomerate diversification. In an earlier chapter, we highlighted the important characteristics that distinguish successful, local companies operating in South and Southeast Asia:

- The companies appear highly diversified; they often undertake unrelated diversification, contravening mainstream theoretical notions.
- The companies have good relationships with the often-enormous public sectors in these countries.
- The companies have very strong familial and informal networks.
- Managers tend to use subjective information as inputs to decision making.

The Salim Group of Indonesia, once the largest of the Overseas Chinese companies, demonstrated these characteristics in this fashion (East Asia Analytical Unit, 1995; Kohut and Cheng, 1996):

- At its peak, Salim had interests in cement, processed foods, flour milling, steel, banking, real estate, investments, pharmaceuticals, information technology, chemicals, shipping, general manufacturing, and vehicle assembly.
- Salim's close ties to the government in its home base of Indonesia were shown by government contracts for flour milling (at an estimated fee of 300 percent of world prices), sharing exclusive rights to import cloves into Indonesia with one other company, and the many Salim companies where the government is a minority shareholder.

These practices would seem to run contrary to Prahalad and Hamel's tenets on developing one's core competency (1990), but they do not. While the Overseas Chinese companies have pursued conglomerate diversification, they instinctively developed, nurtured, and protected their core competencies:

- Their decision-making style
- Their control of information
- Their networks

First, many attribute the rapid growth of the Overseas Chinese businesses in Southeast Asia to their *decision-making style*, especially their speed of decision making (Chu and MacMurray, 1993). This speed, and their dominant control of information (another core competency), facilitate Overseas Chinese efforts to seize business opportunities before competitors sense they exist (Redding, 1986; Haley and Tan, 1996; Haley and Haley, 1997, 1998, 1999; Haley, Haley, and Tan, 2004).

The Overseas Chinese decision-making style that we detailed in Chapter 4 gives them access to various markets (a requirement for a core competency) with scanty data for making analytical decisions. The decision-making style also allows them to take advantage of opportunities such as scarce goods and services, and transfer them to customers, thereby providing the customers with benefits (another requirement for a core competency). Finally, competitors have difficulty imitating this decision-making style (a third requirement for a core competency), especially the multinationals that depend on decision techniques better suited to industrialized markets, and local businessmen who lack the Overseas Chinese managers' hands-on knowledge and business experiences.

Second, the Overseas Chinese's *control over the rich information* they obtain through their networks, a rare commodity in nongovernmental circles, also displays the characteristics of a core competency. The Overseas Chinese managers notably control specialized business information, much of which is considered "insider information" in the West. The Overseas Chinese prosper and produce goods in the informational void that they create and perpetuate. Their information arbitrage offers potential benefits to customers, and competitors have difficulty imitating it. The New Asian Emperors' regional, and increasingly worldwide, business activities endorse their access to a variety of markets. We have indicated the Salim Group's diversity; other examples of Overseas Chinese conglomerate diversification abound. Thailand's Chearavanont Family (CP Group) went from poultry farming into real estate and telecommunications; in the Philippines, Lucio Tan is involved in beer, tobacco, banking, and diversified investments; and in previous chapters, we have sketched the extremely varied investments of Malaysia's Robert Kuok. The Overseas Chinese generally exhibit intense privacy, jealously maintaining secrecy over the sources of information that guide their investments.

Kuok has built a legendary reputation for contributing to and maintaining the informational void in South and Southeast Asia. Some years ago, a leading international investigative agency took an in-depth look at the Kuok Group of companies. After an intensive research effort that spanned six countries, the agency produced a detailed report on the companies' operations—and almost nothing about its management strategies. However, the agency's conclusions about Robert Kuok, whose management acumen binds the companies and gives them focus, were startling (Tanzer, 1997):

Name: Robert Kuok
Political affiliation: unknown
Adversaries: none identified
Litigation: nothing known
Ambitions: not known

For a man whose business empire stretches from Chile to China, and who counts among his friends and partners some of Asia's most powerful politicians and tycoons, Kuok has a remarkable ability to divulge nothing. Over a 50-year career, Kuok has made secrecy both his trademark and his principal asset. He's maintained a wall of secrecy even between himself and the 10 public companies he controls. Five of the listed companies represent the Shangri-La chain and other property investments. They own the bricks and mortar of 27 Shangri-La hotels and resorts around the region; but the management of the hotels—the factor that makes them successful and the area where Kuok's business acumen really counts—remains in the hands of his private company, Shangri-La International Hotel Management. Similar arrangements exist for Kuala Lumpur-listed Federal Flour Mills Bhd, and Perlis Plantations Bhd, through which many of Kuok's edible oil and sugar plantations have been listed.

Finally, for the Overseas Chinese, *their networks* are a core competency. They also furnish potential access to various markets, as demonstrated through the Overseas Chinese ethnic, governmental, and familial contacts. The networks thereby confer power, and power shapes the acquisition and evolution of tacit knowledge. Competitors lack the web of contacts that the Overseas Chinese possess through their networks; consequently, most potential independent local competitors fail to grow large enough to challenge them in the region. Competitors also cannot replicate these textured networks (described in earlier chapters).

The wide networks that the Overseas Chinese use to promote their connections are referred to in Mandarin Chinese as *guanxi,* or influential connections. The practice of *guanxi* leads to a high degree of reliance on trust. *Guanxi's* role also helps to explain why the Overseas Chinese have tended to keep their individual investments in China small or medium-sized; by doing so they can take advantage of their connections with local officials. Projects less than US$30 million do not have to be submitted to Beijing authorities for approval.

For the New Asian Emperors, the "complex harmonization of individual technologies and production skills" that Prahalad and Hamel (1990, p. 84) identified has led to their strategic dominance of Southeast and East Asian business environments. As indicated in previous chapters, neither local competitors nor foreign multinationals can challenge or duplicate the Overseas Chinese ability to make effective strategic decisions, through their networks, in the informational void they maintain.

CHAROEN POKPHAND GROUP

The Classic Network Company

CHAROEN POKPHAND GROUP (CP) has historically been one of the most diversified conglomerates in the Overseas Chinese business world, and many consider it the classic Overseas Chinese network company. One of Thailand's largest companies and one of Asia's first true multinationals, CP's operations span more than 250 companies in 20 countries—largely in Thailand and China but also in Indonesia, Malaysia, India, and Cambodia-—with more than 100,000 employees and sales of US$13 billion. These operations fall under two main business divisions: production and processing, and service.

CP was founded in 1921 as a seed-trading business by two brothers who emigrated from China to Bangkok, Thailand. Today, agriculture constitutes a core business for the group, but CP's breadth remains phenomenal: it operates fast food chains, has a retailing chain of superstores called Lotus (modeled after Wal-Mart), owns China's largest mall, and runs the second largest 7-Eleven franchise in the world after Japan's. It produces PVC, motorcycles, and seeds; is into both agriculture and aquaculture; produces pet food; manages real estate; and operates in the telecommunications and petrochemicals industries.

The Asian financial crisis caught CP short, and the company recognized that its diversification drive had been too ambitious. CP began selling many noncore businesses, including Thai-based Lotus Supercenter to UK's Tesco. Moving into the new century, CP decided to refocus as the "Kitchen to the World," looking at its core agribusiness holdings for future growth. To increase its financial transparency, CP merged 11 of its Thai agribusiness subsidiaries into core group Charoen Pokphand Feedmill by 1999. Charoen Pokphand then became the main vehicle for the now "focused" CP. The company, however, maintained most of its diversified business interests and entered new markets, such as mobile telephony in partnership with Orange in 2000.

Dhanin Chearavanont, CP's chairman, manages hundreds of companies through a large number of partnerships, and many consider him a visionary leader. His ability to manage effectively a large number of relationships, some of which come into conflict with one another, appears to be his greatest skill. He has used his many strategic alliances, joint ventures, and partnerships to expand his company and acquire technology and know-how from the West.

CP's growth has stemmed from management's understanding of Asian culture. It often enters a project through low bids, sometimes willing to accept losses in order to obtain a foothold or establish a crucial new relationship. The group manages its extreme diversification through decentralization. Subsidiaries have great autonomy, and headquarters basically acts as a coordinator of financial resources.

The company has the reputation of being the largest foreign investor in China, though the size and nature of its investments remain unclear. We know that CP Group entered China in 1979 and now has more than 100 joint venture companies in the country, including substantial investments in China's agricultural interior provinces. Continuing in its unique way, in recent years, CP Group moved away from partnerships and joint ventures with major Western and Overseas Chinese companies in their Chinese investments, and has sought to bring smaller Thai companies into projects. CP invested more than US$1 billion in these projects with small companies.

By 2003, *Fortune* magazine labeled Dhanin as one of the "World's Most Powerful Business Leaders" and the only corporate chief in the ASEAN economic zone to be so featured. *Fortune* credited Dhanin with making CP a fully vertically integrated agriculture-to-retail empire, including the world's largest producer of animal feed and one of the top producers of eggs, poultry, and other livestock. In 2008, CP constitutes the only Overseas Chinese business group on Boston Consulting Group's 100 Global Challengers list of multinationals from emerging markets.

   Ghosh and Chan (1994), in their study of strategic-planning behavior among companies in Singapore and Malaysia, classified their planning activities as ad hoc and reactive. The only important, market-related factor that they found centered on the "CEO's personal knowledge of market," which was the fourth most important contributing factor to success in planning. Their findings reflect the highly centralized decision making of the Overseas Chinese (Redding, 1986; Haley and Tan, 1996): specifically, the "CEO's personal knowledge" of the market assumes importance, not the company's or the marketing manager's. The Overseas Chinese went into two crises with these traditional strategic-planning behaviors: the 1997 financial crisis and the 2002–03 SARS epidemic. The two crises whipsawed Southeast and East Asian economies unmercifully in the late 20th and early 21st centuries. Many countries that escaped the 1997 financial crisis could not evade the SARS epidemic and its effects. The next chapters explore the evolution of Overseas Chinese management styles as a response to the crises, the strengths and weakness of this style, and implications for their stakeholders.

PART III

The Implications for Business

CHAPTER 6

In the Aftermath of the Asian Crises: Revolution or Evolution?

Remember that you are responsible to your ancestors, not just to yourself. Our ancestors are not honored by compromise; they are honored by responsible behavior and hard work.

—Tan Suang U, to his son in Bataan

We researched a large portion of the business literature on the Overseas Chinese, discussed our ideas with many of the community's patriarchs (including some of the New Asian Emperors), advised many of their companies and their competitors, and studied them for several years. In our final two chapters, we assess the business groups' evolution in the aftermath of the Asian financial and SARS crises. We synthesize our findings to discuss the implications of the Overseas Chinese strategic planning styles and delineate their comparative advantages and disadvantages. We also present a strategic-planning model for success in competing and cooperating with the Overseas Chinese.

First, we trace the chronology of the Asian financial crisis and SARS in the Overseas Chinese groups' competitive environments. Next, we discuss how the business groups evolved in response to the crises. In the ensuing sections, we elaborate on the competitive advantages and disadvantages of the Overseas Chinese manner of

doing business. In the next chapter, we elaborate on the implications that the Overseas Chinese decision-making style has for the
conduct of business in Southeast Asia. We close with a short discussion of the future influence of the Overseas Chinese on practice
and research, and on how to plan for success in competing against
and with them.

The Path of Destruction

The Asian financial crisis of 1997–1998 and the SARS epidemic of
2002–2004 created long-lasting environmental changes and forced
both reevaluation and restructuring of the Overseas Chinese business groups. In this section we track the crises and their effects on
competitive business environments in Asia.

The 1997–1998 Asian financial crisis

The Asian financial crisis took place after over a decade of tremendous growth. From the 1960s through 1997, including previous
downturns, the countries of Southeast Asia were the fastest-growing
economic region in the world. Additionally, unlike China today,
Southeast Asia's ASEAN countries had served as engines of growth
and employment around the world. Indeed, Southeast Asia constituted the only economic region in the world, other than the U.S., to
run a trade deficit. Most people view the crisis as beginning on July
2, when Thailand allowed its currency to float after the National
Bank conceded that a disastrous investment policy could not support the baht or guarantee the solvency of financial institutions
(Nanto, 1998; Haley, Haley, and Tan, 2004; Haley and Richter,
2002). As the chronology given here shows, Thailand, Indonesia,
and the East Asian economic powerhouse, South Korea, took especially hard hits.

Chronology of the 1997 Asian Financial Crisis

Early May   Japan hints that it might raise interest rates to defend the yen. The threat never materializes but shifts global investors' perceptions. Investors begin to sell Southeast Asian currencies, which sets off a tumble both in currencies and in local stock markets.

July

2   After using $33 billion in foreign exchange to support it, Thailand announces a managed float of the baht. The Philippines intervenes to defend its peso.

18   IMF approves an extension of credit to the Philippines of $1.1 billion.

24   Asian currencies fall dramatically. Malaysian Prime Minister Mahathir Mohamad attacks "rogue speculators" and later points to financier George Soros.

August

13–14   The Indonesian rupiah comes under severe pressure. Indonesia abolishes its system of managing the exchange rate within a specific band.

20   The IMF announces a $17.2 billion support package for Thailand, including $3.9 billion from the IMF itself.

28   Asian stock markets plunge. Manila falls by 9.3 percent, Jakarta by 4.5 percent.

September

4   The peso, Malaysian ringgit, and rupiah continue to fall.

October

8   The rupiah hits a record low; Indonesia says it will seek IMF assistance.

14   Thailand announces a package to strengthen its financial sector.

20–23   The Hong Kong dollar comes under speculative attack; Hong Kong aggressively defends its currency. The Hong Kong stock market drops, while Wall Street and other stock markets also take severe hits.

28+   The value of the Korean won drops as investors sell Korean stocks.

November

5   The IMF announces a stabilization package of about
            US$40 billion for Indonesia. The U.S. pledges a
            standby credit of US$3 billion.

3–24   A Japanese brokerage firm (Sanyo Securities), its
            largest securities firm (Yamaichi Securities), and the
            tenth largest bank (Hokkaido Takushoku) collapse.

21   South Korea announces that it will seek IMF support.

25   At the APEC Summit, leaders of the 18 Asia Pacific
            economies endorse a framework to cope with the
            financial crisis.

December

3   Korea and the IMF agree on a $57 billion support package.

5   Malaysia imposes tough reforms to reduce its balance-
            of-payments deficit.

25   The IMF and others supply US$10 billion in loans to
            South Korea.

1998

January

6   Indonesia unveils a new budget that fails to meet the IMF's
            austerity conditions. The rupiah's value drops further.

8   The IMF and South Korea agree to a 90-day rollover of
            short-term debt.

12   Peregrine Investments Holdings of Hong Kong
            collapses. Japan discloses that its banks carry about
            US$580 billion in bad or questionable loans.

15   The IMF and Indonesia sign an agreement on
            strengthening economic reforms.

29   South Korea and 13 international banks agree to
            convert US$24 billion in short-term debt, due in
            March 1998, into government-backed loans.

31   South Korea orders 10 of 14 ailing merchant banks to close.

February

2   The sense of crisis in Asia ebbs. Stock markets
            continue recovery.

Source: Note, 1998.

TABLE 6.1: *Economic Effects of the 1997 Financial Crisis: The Collapse of the Currencies and Stock Markets Between June 11, 1997, and January 22, 1998*

	Thailand	Indonesia	S. Korea
Change in exchange rate	38%	81%	50%
Change in stock market	26%	40%	30%

Source: Nanto, 1998.

The crisis had devastating effects on the economies of Thailand, Indonesia, and South Korea. The aforementioned Peregrine Fund's collapse in Hong Kong occurred because of losses in Indonesia. As Table 6.1 encapsulates, the crisis devastated currencies: the Indonesian rupiah plunged 81 percent in about six months, the Korean won fell 50 percent, and the Thai baht fell 38 percent. Their stock markets fared little better. Yet, as we will show, most of the Overseas Chinese business groups, though battered, did survive and even prosper.

The 2002–2004 SARS crisis

The SARS epidemic began in Guangdong province, China, in 2002. Before finally winding down in 2004, it threw Southeast and East Asia into an economic crisis that the World Bank dubbed as the worst since 1997 (Haley, Haley, and Tan, 2004). Some countries and industries fared worse than others. Estimates of the cost of the SARS epidemic ranged from US$10 billion to US$30 billion, causing the World Trade Organization in 2003 to revise downward its original projection of 5 percent growth in global trade to 2.5–3.0 percent growth (Robertson, 2003).

Table 6.2 sketches the estimated costs to various East and Southeast Asian economies. Industries such as tourism and real estate took the brunt of the whipping. As an entrepôt and travel hub, Singapore suffered more economically during the SARS epidemic than during the Asian financial crisis.

TABLE 6.2: *The Economic Impact of SARS*

Economies	Estimated 2003 GDP Growth Before SARS (Percentage Points)	Estimated 2003 GDP Growth If SARS Lasts Two Quarters (Percentage Points)	Estimated Reduction in Annual GDP Levels If SARS Lasts Two Quarters (US$ Billions)
East Asia	**5.6**	**4.7**	**20.7**
PRC	7.3	7.0	5.8
Hong Kong	2.0	−1.4	6.6
South Korea	4.0	3.5	3.0
Taiwan	3.7	1.8	5.3
Southeast Asia	**4.0**	**2.5**	**7.7**
Indonesia	3.4	2.3	2.0
Malaysia	4.3	2.9	1.3
Philippines	4.0	3.2	0.6
Singapore	2.3	0.7	2.0
Thailand	5.0	3.4	1.8

Source: Asian Development, ADB News Release No. 065/03.

Despite its ferocity and economic costs, the SARS crisis proved a short-lived stochastic shock. Table 6.3 outlines the chronology of the SARS epidemic.

Medically, SARS seemed a relatively mild epidemic. For example, people contract pneumonia much more easily. By way of comparison, in 2002 Hong Kong suffered 1,755 cases of SARS with a 17 percent mortality rate; simultaneously, the country had 13,480 cases of pneumonia with a 17.5 percent mortality rate (Siu and Wong, 2005). Yet the SARS epidemic demonstrates that short-lived crises can create economic and social havoc. The epidemic also shows that a major pandemic could devastate the Overseas Chinese business groups and the Southeast Asian economies in which they

TABLE 6.3: *Chronology of the 2003 SARS Epidemic*

April 2	Travel advisory for Hong Kong, China, and Guangdong.
April 23	Travel advisory extended to Beijing, Shanxi, and Toronto.
April 28	Vietnam removed from list of affected countries.
April 29	Travel advisory lifted for Toronto.
May 8	Travel advisory extended to Tianjin, Inner Mongolia, and Taipei.
May 21	Travel advisory extended to all of Taipei, China.
May 23	Travel advisory lifted for Hong Kong, China, and Guangdong.
May 30	Singapore removed from list of areas with local transmission of SARS.
June 13	Travel advisory lifted on Tianjin, Inner Mongolia, and Shanxi.
June 17	Travel advisory lifted on Taipei, China.
June 23	Hong Kong, China removed from list of areas with local transmission of SARS.
June 24	Travel advisory lifted on Beijing; Beijing removed from list of areas with local transmission of SARS.
July 5	Taipei, China removed from list of areas with local transmission of SARS.

Source: Asian Development Bank.

flourish. The next section discusses how the Overseas Chinese business groups reacted to the crises.

The Post-crises Evolution of Overseas Chinese Business Groups

The Asian crises outlined in the previous section forced the regional governments and the Overseas Chinese groups to reevaluate and restructure. Although the financial crisis highlighted the region's and business groups' institutional and structural weaknesses, the stochastic shock of SARS revealed the problems associated with concentrating business activities solely in East and Southeast Asia.

The Overseas Chinese business groups also displayed resilience by bouncing back from both crises.

In the wake of the financial crisis, banks and other financial institutions quickly became insolvent. Interest rates and exchange rates skyrocketed. Many of the Overseas Chinese business groups' heavily indebted industrial companies went bankrupt. Unemployed people flooded the streets. The financial crisis most directly affected Thailand, Indonesia, and Malaysia; yet other Asian countries—including Singapore, which relied heavily on intraregion trade—tottered as well. The SARS crisis had a short-term shock impact on the business groups, which disrupted supply chains. Many business groups renewed their efforts to diversify outside Southeast and East Asia into South Asia and Europe. The crises therefore serve as a prism to understand the evolution of the Overseas Chinese business groups.

First, despite the hardships associated with the crises, most Overseas Chinese business groups remained intact and displayed resilience in the face of external shocks. Many expected the crises to decimate debt-ridden business groups in the afflicted countries. Analysts and Western policymakers argued for post-crisis economic and financial restructuring programs initiated by the International Monetary Fund (IMF), and for Anglo-Saxon governance models for the business groups instituted by the World Bank. Yet most Overseas Chinese business groups in the region survived the adverse conditions. Many remained intact and some even prospered. In countries less affected by the crisis, such as Taiwan, the groups expanded.

Our detailed interviews with Overseas Chinese CEOs (some of whom we identify in the Appendix), both before and after the crises, indicate that the crises and foreign, extraneous influences resulted in internal upheaval. Yet the Overseas Chinese business groups' fundamental practices persisted because they generated real benefits, matched institutional environments, were socially and culturally embedded, and drew governmental protection. Globalization theorists (for example Ohmae, 1990) have argued that global convergence of markets and business organization will occur through intensified global competition. Even so, the Overseas Chinese business groups' post-crisis restructuring indicates that changes because of globalization are more evolutionary than revolutionary (Campbell, 2004) and along the lines of those forecasted by Haley, Haley, and Tan (2004).

Second, our interviews show that the Overseas Chinese business groups evolved in divergent fashion in response to the crisis. The government in each country perceived discrete problems and had its own ability to implement change. Business groups fiercely resisted any changes that would undermine their resources and power bases. The prevailing institutional infrastructures, culture, social norms, and ethnic conflicts in each country further constrained development of business groups and their institutional environments.

The crises did not directly affect Taiwan and Singapore. Taiwanese groups have continued to expand and diversify, especially after deregulation; private companies now have unfettered access to previously blocked domestic sectors. In contrast, the Singaporean government emphasized divestment, foreign acquisition, and professional governance. In Singapore, the distinctions between the state and private sector have blurred. Many state-owned enterprises (SOEs) approximate business groups run by professional managers. When the financial crisis began, the government initiated restructuring to combat weak corporate governance and lack of market discipline. But the pace of divestment by the SOEs and banking groups has evolved gradually, showing some inertia.

Overseas Chinese business groups in Malaysia, Thailand, and Indonesia showed no coherent pattern of restructuring after the crises (see Chang, 2006, for a detailed discussion). Rather, indigenous business groups with close governmental ties benefited from the crises by acquiring failed businesses without these ties. Conflicts between indigenous peoples and the Overseas Chinese further thwarted the restructuring process; cronyism and corruption have also delayed the building of institutional infrastructures. For example, the Malaysian government failed to implement various structural reforms to enhance transparency and accountability. Similarly in Thailand, despite legal measures to remodel the country's institutional environment, the business groups' ownership structures remain intact. Nonetheless, many Overseas Chinese business groups lost their financial base in Thailand, limiting their ability to obtain funds easily. In Indonesia, business groups are still struggling. Since the Asian Crisis, some groups, such as the Salim Group (see Dieleman, 2007), have transformed their corporate structure and survived the turmoil. Others have lost control over their company or struggled to keep control. Political connections appear to be one of the factors separating winners from losers.

Many country-specific institutional arrangements related to organized labor, business, and electoral politics have constrained the effects of globalization (Campbell, 2004; Whitley, 2008). The Anglo-Saxon model of corporate governance has not emerged as the gold standard for Overseas Chinese businesses. Instead, the Overseas Chinese business groups appear to contribute to a divergent capitalism (Whitley, 1999) that incorporates distinct combinations of markets and economic organizations in each country and adaptation to their institutional environment.

Third, the countries that the Overseas Chinese call home have followed various trajectories after the crises. Several affected countries changed their institutional environment after the financial crisis. They enhanced corporate governance and tightened capital-market supervision. These changes will have long-term ramifications for business groups' further evolution. Southeast Asia has recently had several years of strong growth (see Figure 6.1). Government finances have improved. However, as we showed in Chapter 4, the informational black hole continues and business groups still control information contributing to their tacit knowledge and skilful performance.

Finally, Southeast Asian restructuring efforts failed to alter significantly the institutional features contributing to weakness among the Overseas Chinese groups. *The Economist* (2008) noted that the region's five main economies—Indonesia, Malaysia, the Philippines, Singapore, and Thailand, with 570 million people—possess almost no world-class companies (we previously identified Charoen Pokphand Group as an exception) or global consumer brands (other than Singapore Airlines). Although Taiwan's export-led growth originated

FIGURE 6.1: *Average Annual Percentage of Real GDP Growth*

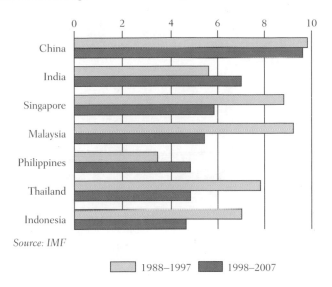

Source: IMF

1988–1997 ■ 1998–2007

from indigenous companies making globally competitive goods with proprietary technologies, foreign companies still manufacture much of Southeast Asia's high value exports. A recent study by the Boston Consulting Group (BCG) of the 100 largest multinationals from emerging economies (a category excluding Singapore) contained only five from the whole region. By contrast, Brazil had 13 (see Figure 6.2). In banking, the region has some impressive contenders, such as Singapore's OCBC and Malaysia's Public Bank, which are expanding beyond their borders. But now they must contend with China's huge and increasingly muscle-flexing banks as well as Western banks with deep roots in the region, such as HSBC and Standard Chartered.

For reasons we discuss in later sections, the Overseas Chinese companies lack size in a global economy where scale economies matter. Despite the lessons from SARS, not many Overseas Chinese business groups have wandered beyond their home market. However, because of ASEAN's fragmentation, many Overseas Chinese companies do not have a sizeable home market from which to build world-beating businesses. ASEAN's members still conduct three times as much trade with nonmembers as they do among themselves. The

FIGURE 6.2: *Number of BCG 100 Global Challengers*

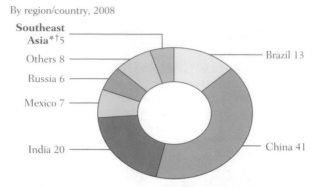

By region/country, 2008

Southeast Asia*†5
Others 8
Russia 6
Mexico 7
India 20
Brazil 13
China 41

*In Southeast Asia:

Company	Country	Main business
Indofood Sukses Makmur	Indonesia	Food & drink
Malaysia International Shipping Co.	Malaysia	Shipping
Petronas	Malaysia	Fossil fuels
Charoen Pokphand Foods	Thailand	Food & drink
Thai Union Frozen Products	Thailand	Food & drink

†*Excluding Singapore*
Source: Boston Consulting Group

Asian financial crisis and SARS have spurred the cutting of internal tariffs, but as a 2004 McKinsey & Company report noted, product standards and other nontariff barriers often differ among ASEAN countries, forcing manufacturers to make small production runs for each country. These factors lower the competitiveness of the Overseas Chinese companies, as well as of multinational companies operating in the region. The next sections home in on the competitive advantages and disadvantages of Overseas Chinese businesses.

Competitive Advantages of the Overseas Chinese

As we identified in the previous section, many Overseas Chinese companies have improved their profitability since the 1997–1998 crisis. YTL, a Malaysian company, is one of the groups. Dominant in construction, the company also owns a British water firm, Wessex Water; operates hotels and up-market shopping malls; runs a high-speed rail link from central Kuala Lumpur to the city's airport; and owns a chain of power stations. Its founder, Yeoh Tiong Lay, built a giant construction business with state contracts in the country's early post-independence period. In the 1990s, when his friend Mahathir Mohamad served as prime minister, the company obtained concessions to generate electricity using subsidized gas from the state oil company, which the state's electricity company had to buy. The founder's son, Francis Yeoh, who now runs the group, insisted that it does not rest on its laurels. YTL has delivered, he argued, a 55 percent annual compounded growth in profits since the mid-1980s, and now earns 70 percent of revenues outside Malaysia (*Economist*, 2008). On February 22, 2008, it declared a profit for the six months to December 31, 2007, of 688 million ringgit (US$202 million), 24 percent more than a year before. Yeoh stated that the company's core competence included building and maintaining infrastructural assets of first-world quality at third-world prices. He also viewed the group's hotels and shopping malls as "unregulated infrastructure." In the future, Yeoh foresaw opportunities from applying Wessex Water's skills at cleaning up rivers to Asia's murky waterways. However, some sizeable Chinese water-treatment companies would also pursue those same contracts. Currently, Wessex Water is making profits in England but has not tested its potential to become a global leader. This section explores some competitive advantages of Overseas Chinese companies such as YTL.

There are many opinions on the competitive advantages of the Overseas Chinese. Drawing on the core competencies that we identified in the previous chapter, we argue that four factors give the Overseas Chinese competitive advantage in their business dealings in Southeast and East Asia:

- Speed
- Knowledge
- *Guanxi*
- Empowerment

Speed

Kwek Leng Beng, who took over the Hong Leong Group from his father, said:

> I have seen both the old man's style and Western-style man-agement. The latter is bogged down by many layers of the decision-making process. Consequently, you lose speed, and as a result, you also lose the deal. For example, it took us just 48 hours to tender for Grand Hyatt Taipei. You can say that I have incorporated into my management style and business approach the best of both worlds (*Asiamoney, 1994*).

Their vaunted speed of decision and action flows from their deci-sion-making style, a core competency of the Overseas Chinese that we previously identified. Many Western observers note speed as the primary competitive advantage of the Overseas Chinese. When asked about their greatest competitive advantage, many of the Overseas Chinese will also mention speed. Stan Shih, chairman and founder of Acer Computers, told us, "We believe in doing things quickly" and "We implement and change things quickly. It's all implementation in the market place."

Both Western and Overseas Chinese decision-making styles accept the existence of uncertainty and try to minimize it. However, Western strategic decision making depends heavily on quantifi-able and measurable data. Western managers often become sty-mied when they confront environments that do not generate the data they require and to which they have become accustomed, delaying strategic decisions for many Western companies. The Overseas Chinese managers can arrive quickly at strategic decisions with minimal information, primarily through use of subjective data, speeding strategic decisions for their company. Moreover, many strategic decisions of Western companies go through hierarchical levels that do not exist in Overseas Chinese companies. Consequently, the Overseas Chinese companies have a nimbleness that most major Western companies envy.

Knowledge

Their knowledge stems from control of information, a core competency of the Overseas Chinese that we previously identified. The Overseas Chinese have recognized their competitive advantage and actively sought to monopolize sources of special market and business information. Historically, their manner of conducting business has involved developing their sources of information to the greatest extent possible. Networking supplies their market research, and talks with friends and sifting of experiences serve as their analyses. Combined, these two activities give the Overseas Chinese the input and analysis necessary for informed decision making. The Overseas Chinese, however, can create and maintain a monopoly over this knowledge relatively easily.

The Overseas Chinese create their competitive advantages in market and business information in two ways. First, they practice an exclusionary style of business. This does not mean that all the Overseas Chinese networks exclude non-Chinese. Contrary to popular opinion, the Overseas Chinese do have people of other nationalities in their networks and inner circles. Indeed, close inspection of the Overseas Chinese networks and companies in Southeast Asia indicates that both include many non-Chinese members. Like other businesspeople, the Overseas Chinese look for trustworthy, upright, hard-working, honest, loyal individuals who possess talents needed by their circle of friends and associates. However, the Overseas Chinese style of business excludes nonassociates from possessing the same advantages that the Overseas Chinese and their associates have. Competitors and nonassociates find they simply cannot obtain the quality and quantity of knowledge needed to compete on a more equal footing.

Second, the Overseas Chinese maintain a competitive advantage in knowledge through inaction. If the more economically advanced Southeast Asian countries' business communities desired freer and greater availability of market and business information, they would lobby their governments and probably obtain its release. Indeed, the Southeast Asian governments do supply data for the markets; but at least two types of data exist: freely available data, which therefore have little competitive consequence, and "special data." Various Southeast Asian networks generally enjoy exclusive access to the special data. Because these networks prefer to maintain their monopoly over the local markets' special data, they do not lobby their governments for a level playing field.

Most regional business deals also involve some elements of government licensing or concessions, which both parties prefer to keep private. Consequently, secrecy permeates Overseas Chinese business dealings and processes. In 1991, Robert Kuok wrote a letter to the *Far Eastern Economic Review* with reasons for this secrecy and for his refusing interviews with the news magazine: "The average Chinese is publicity shy for various reasons, is averse to washing linen in public, and, consequently, also averse to dealing with the media" (Friedland, 1991, p. 46). As Joe Studwell noted (2007), this reticence did not prevent Kuok from buying the *South China Morning Post* in 1993. Not surprisingly, Studwell (2007), in his book *The Asian Godfathers,* did not appear to have obtained interviews with any of the Overseas Chinese tycoons that he so caustically profiled (although he did mention many undisclosed sources from the business groups).

Guanxi

Guanxi (a Mandarin term, with no exact English translation, which includes concepts of trust and the ability and knowledge of how to present uprightness to build relationships) stems from their networks, a core competency of the Overseas Chinese that we previously identified. The ability to generate trust, and to judge who among others appears worthy of trust, constitutes a true competitive advantage for the Overseas Chinese in Southeast Asia. Though Westerners obviously have the ability to judge others—and to generate trust among others—uprightness forms one of the most culturally specific aspects of Overseas Chinese business culture.

Guanxi gives Overseas Chinese an important competitive advantage over Western companies: a discrepancy in the availability of information between Western companies and Overseas Chinese companies. The large, publicly held Western companies that most often enter Southeast and East Asia dispense freely available information on their operations and strategies. If a company develops an exemplary reputation, it becomes freely available knowledge. Alternatively, if a company develops a reputation for having difficulty in dealings with Asian partners and customers, this too becomes freely available knowledge or knowledge the networks can obtain through their contacts.

Conversely, as we indicated in the previous chapter, most people without local contacts have difficulty obtaining knowledge on Overseas Chinese companies. Most of the companies are closely held and information is not widely available or published, especially in Western circles. Many Westerners have no knowledge of the Asia-based publications or sources that would furnish valuable sources of information or strategic leads. Due to the closely guarded privacy of most Overseas Chinese, and their proclivity to share information only among their own networks of friends and associates, most Overseas Chinese businesspersons do not divulge information about local markets or business situations to strangers. Trust usually develops through years of socializing and doing business with people. Also, Overseas Chinese generally judge individuals, not companies; they direct their loyalty and trust accordingly toward individuals rather than companies.

CHINA AND THE OVERSEAS CHINESE

Reaching out Through the Networks

THOUSANDS OF BUSINESS delegations leave China each year for the Asia Pacific to contact local ethnic Chinese communities and local Chinese Chambers of Commerce in their quest for investment for their home area in China. Although specific figures are lacking, the *huaqiao,* or Overseas Chinese community, is among the biggest groups of investors in China. Through family and clan, regional, and dialect ties, the Overseas Chinese created an empire without borders that generated an estimated GNP of around US$1.5 trillion in 2002—third after the U.S. and Japan. Some of that money has been pouring back into the mainland since the Chinese economy opened in 1978. After the Asian crises, according to World Bank estimates the ASEAN countries with the largest concentrations of Overseas Chinese—Singapore, Thailand, the Philippines, Indonesia, and Malaysia—have continued to pour more than US$4 billion annually into China.

Traditionally, Overseas Chinese have preferred to do business with people of their own dialect or clan. In Malaysia, on the booming Penang waterfront, seven old piers represent the clan-based *gongsi* (syndicates) that used to trade exclusively with their own kind. Typically, New Asian Emperor Li Ka-shing, who was born in 1928 in the sleepy city of Chaozhou (Chiuchow in Cantonese) in southeast Guangdong, has made many financial investments and commitments to his ancestral region, including US$13 million to various Chaozhou charities and US$152 million for the founding of Shantou University in the nearby city of Shantou. "I'm a Chiuchow person," Li told friends in China in the early 1990s; "I'll earn money elsewhere and bring it back home."

Many delegations originate from specific parts of China and frequently attempt to contact their former compatriots living abroad. For example, in 1994 a business delegation from Fuzhou in Fujian province visited the timber and logging city of Sibu in Malaysia's Sarawak. Sibu has a high concentration of Overseas Chinese who originate from Fuzhou. The New Asian Emperors have not forgotten home.

Despite their ethnic and financial ties, the *huaqiao* rarely exercise the political influence in China that they do in their Southeast Asian home countries. Indeed, Wang Gung Wu called it "eunuch wealth," or wealth that cannot translate naturally into political power. The Overseas Chinese acquire their wealth in an environment devoid of legal and institutional guarantees. Therefore, just as political connections confer wealth, so governments can snatch it away. Regional governments and rival indigenous groups also suspect the Overseas Chinese of having pro-Beijing allegiances. To avoid such accusations, Overseas Chinese often respect the wishes of the local government and seldom invest in China solely for ethnically inspired reasons (though these do sway final decisions).

Empowerment

As the Overseas Chinese networks of companies have grown, their people have spread globally; yet their organizational structures remain flat, and in many ways lean. The centers have retained substantial control. The dispersed, subsidiary units remain largely autonomous, but with strong supporting links to the centers. The numerous hierarchical levels found in many Western firms and some Japanese do not exist. The subsidiary units' key managers are trusted employees; they wheel and deal and expand the subsidiaries within the constraints of the centers' vision. Western management circles classify the Overseas Chinese subsidiary managers' authority and actions as empowerment.

Overseas Union Enterprise's Thio Gim Hock (of Lippo Group) explicitly emphasized empowerment when he told us, "Many Chinese owner/CEOs get their hands on a project and get into the details. Stephen [Riady] is very different. He establishes a macro policy that gives guidance but leaves the details to the professional managers. The operations and functions are all in the hands of the managers. It puts pressure on us to perform, to really develop a project that is marketable—that is coherent and sound. He has final say on the project, but he doesn't interfere with the details." The best of the Overseas Chinese companies have empowered their managers for years; thus the business networks grew rapidly.

In the Chinese networks, the subsidiaries look to headquarters for guidance on policies, for directional thrust or vision, and for financial support. The financial relationships approximate those of venture-capital companies and their clients. Headquarters supports field operations and approves general plans but transcends day-to-day operations and decision making.

The companies in Overseas Chinese networks exude a paternalistic culture. Employees receive substantial bonuses when they produce good results. Lifelong employment constitutes the norm. Senior managers often consider the best, most talented, and most

LI & FUNG'S JOHN WAYNE STRUCTURE

L I & FUNG HAS GROWN into the world's largest trading organization on the basis of the organizational principal that selective uniformity and centralized control grant effective independence of action. In an interview with us, CEO Victor Fung labeled this his "John Wayne organizational structure" and exhorted his line managers to behave as John Waynes. In his most memorable film roles, Li & Fung's CEO argued, Wayne played fiercely independent, highly determined, and driven people who achieved their goals through any honorable means. Victor Fung actively seeks this type of manager. Such people, he told us, "if they did not work for Li & Fung, would rather start their own business than work for a more traditionally structured company. They must be able to operate on their own, without strict supervision; they must be entrepreneurial."

Li & Fung structures its trading operations around customers and product markets. Each John Wayne manages 30 to 40 people who focus on specific customers' needs within product markets Li & Fung serves, primarily textiles, toys, health and beauty, and importation of packaged foods into their home markets. The company hopes to become its customers' extended supply chain and employs John Waynes to make it so.

This structure evolved at Li & Fung by dint of the large number of transactions in which the company engages. A centralized structure failed to manage transactions effectively while simultaneously interfacing with customers to offer the rapid and thorough service that has distinguished Li & Fung. Each John Wayne structure enompasses a corporate profit center and has complete authority in marketing, customer service, product selection

> and development, purchasing, logistics, distribution, and sales. Corporate finance and information technology (IT) remain the only centralized functions. The John Waynes must live within management's funding constraints or else justify the need for additional funding. Structural lubricants include extensive investment in IT and enforced uniformity of all IT documents and corporate communications. All corporate communications occur in English, and consistent IT forms and devices permeate Li & Fung.

upright employees for potential partnerships in new businesses they fund. Such benefits hinder Western multinationals from hiring away the best of the Overseas Chinese companies' employees. We next discuss some of their attendant competitive disadvantages.

Competitive Disadvantages of the Overseas Chinese

As Lao Tzu would have recognized, many of the competitive disadvantages of the Overseas Chinese stem from their competitive advantages. The disadvantages that we perceive them to have are:

- Home turf only
- Susceptibility to blind-siding
- Proprietary capabilities
- Family limits
- Lack of professionalization

Home turf only

The home-turf-only disadvantage stems from their control of information, a core competency of the Overseas Chinese that we previously identified. In some industries, the Overseas Chinese appear extremely competitive regardless of where they operate. For example, the Overseas Chinese have proven extremely successful in property development and the hotel and resort investments that they make. However, the Overseas Chinese frequently have trouble when they move into manufacturing industries. For example, Li Ka-shing, called Superman in Hong Kong for his skills in spotting business opportunities, failed badly in two mid-1980s forays into Western markets. In Canada, he bought Husky Oil Ltd. and incurred losses of US$183 million before he finally turned it around in 1993; and in Britain, his company Hutchison set up a cordless-phone operation called Rabbit and suffered losses of US$183 million before finally selling it. Similarly, Creative Technology, with 70 percent market share worldwide in the sound-card market, has historically done poorly with new product launches in the U.S. market, though half its sales occur in the U.S.

The Overseas Chinese companies often fail in the West because they depend on an intimate knowledge of their business and their market for their decisions. Consequently, the Overseas Chinese managers come to expect, and depend on, an advantage in the quantity and quality of strategic information. When they leave their home market, they lose their access to this special business information we identified. Thus, historically, they have done poorly away from home turf and have not posed a serious threat to move into Western multinationals' home markets as the Japanese companies did. However, Western companies can no longer count on this advantage. The founding generations of Overseas Chinese businessmen are retiring and handing over the reins to their heirs. Our interviews with these heirs reveal that unlike past generations, they have training in the traditional business practices of the Overseas Chinese, as well as in the best business schools of the West. Many have significant experience in Western multinationals and have the preparation to live and conduct business in both worlds. Many of the heirs appear to be formidable opponents, as we discuss later.

Susceptibility to blind-siding

Trust assumes great importance in network economic systems. The susceptibility to blind-siding stems from the Overseas Chinese networks having trust as a core competency. Unlike in the industrial West, trust among the Overseas Chinese does not derive from consistently enforced and reliable legal systems; it stems from personal trust-based systems. Any trust-based system such as that of the Overseas Chinese networks is susceptible to blind-siding. Though trust reaps enormous economic benefits (Fukuyama, 1995), it exposes those employing it as a primary competitive tool to significant losses.

During and after the financial crisis, and throughout difficulties with the post-Suharto Indonesian governments, many Overseas Chinese companies lived up to the highest standards of Chinese ethics. Salim Group (Dieleman, 2007) and RGM formed two such companies. Regardless of the tremendous difficulties they encountered, they worked closely with their lenders to resolve their debt obligations. Living up to ethical standards can generate immense benefits for companies and individuals. Sukanto Tanoto, RGM's founder, told us, "We maintained close dialogue and continued to service our debts based on agreement reached with the majority of the leaders. Had we not done so, we could not have grown as we did once the crisis had passed." However, not all Overseas Chinese companies behaved similarly.

The collapse of Peregrine Investments' holdings presents an example of blind-siding and its effects. A high flier before the financial crisis, Peregrine grew in 10 years to become the largest home-grown investment house in Asia outside of Japan. Peregrine's collapse came after the Indonesian rupiah was allowed to float and became seriously devalued. Because of the devaluation, a major Indonesian debtor, Steady Safe, could not repay the US$260 million bridge loan it owed to Peregrine. The company could not reclaim any of the loans, and investigators could not determine what happened to the money. Given the economic difficulties in Indonesia, one can comprehend that Steady Safe's bond issue and loan went sour (despite support from the Suharto family); however, the complete disappearance of US$260 million clearly indicates a breakdown in the trust-based relationships of the Overseas Chinese. Because the networks draw so completely on trust, any significant trend toward blind-siding can bring the system crashing down. The end result was Peregrine's collapse. Its directors, and especially Philip Tose and Francis Leung, ensured that Peregrine met all its own obligations and helped their employees find new jobs. In doing so, they maintained their personal reputation, and in 2000, Leung rebuilt Peregrine Investment's successor, BNP Prime Peregrine Capital, Ltd., into the fourth largest investment bank in Asia outside Japan (Balfour, 2000).

Poor proprietary capabilities

Poor proprietary capabilities stem from the sometimes reactive nature of their strategic decision-making style. As we indicated in the previous chapter, many have noted (see Ghosh and Chan, 1994) that the average Overseas Chinese company appears reactive. This characteristic holds true for the average Western company too. However, the major Western multinationals have only recently begun to sell their products in the home markets of Overseas Chinese companies; and though relatively new to the environment, and in many instances struggling, Western multinationals have the brand-name recognition and technological prowess that many Overseas Chinese companies lack. The Overseas Chinese companies' reactive nature sometimes hinders them from aggressively building their name and developing their technologies. Stan Shih of Acer recognized this major potential problem when he told us, "Branding is natural to an American company but is unusual in this part of the world." Few Overseas Chinese companies are struggling to build their brand equity within the region as fiercely as Acer.

McDonald's is the best-known restaurant in Asia; Coke and Pepsi are the best-known soft drinks. Procter & Gamble, the market leader in China, holds a 50 percent share in China's shampoo market— even at three times the price of local products. The U.S., European, and Japanese giants Procter & Gamble, Unilever, and Kao have started waging their battle of the detergents. The failure of many of the Overseas Chinese companies to establish brand recognition or loyalty even in their home market, or to exercise a technological edge, may seriously prevent their establishing a global market niche against the Japanese and Western consumer-products companies.

Like brand equity, many Overseas Chinese companies also fail to perceive the value of home-grown technology. Many of their managers believe in buying or copying technology, or if necessary, licensing products. The Southeast and East Asian economies, in which most of the Overseas Chinese companies maintain their operations, have leapfrogged from centuries of primarily village-oriented subsistence economies to decades of fantastic growth. Consequently, the dominant companies are only now accepting marketing concepts, and they often ignore the value of product development outside of copying established, generally mature products. Overseas Chinese companies very rarely develop new technologies, with Acer the best-known exception to the rule.

Family limits

The family limits on Overseas Chinese companies originate from the Chinese business approximating the Chinese family. Traditionally, when the family can no longer furnish the skills necessary, an Overseas Chinese company reaches the limits of its growth and begins to decline. In actuality, nonfamily members can become, for all practical purposes, part of the family by showing their worth within the business, so the limitation is not as restrictive as it initially seems. However, once a company grows beyond the size where it can be run as a family, and once an authoritarian patriarch can no longer efficiently centralize decision making himself, the family has to make changes in how they run their business.

Our interviews with the New Asian Emperors (see the Appendix) reveal that several Overseas Chinese companies have already encountered the problem of family limits, and many companies have successfully adapted. However, when an emperor passes on or retires, the succession period will pose a significant threat for many of the great Overseas Chinese empires. Some companies appear to be making the transition smoothly, such as United Overseas Bank and Wuthelam Group of Singapore, and Hutchison Whampoa/Cheung Kong Holdings of Hong Kong; but for many others, the succession promises difficulties. The Wanglees of Thailand have shown that despite the biting Chinese prophecy of wealth not surviving to the third generation, successions can go well.

Family limits directly affect the Overseas Chinese companies' ability to grow and therefore their ability to garner economies of scale. Indeed, as Figure 6.3 shows, productivity in China and India is growing much faster than in Southeast Asia. East Asia overtook the region in output per worker in 2000 and has continued to power ahead. As we outlined in previous chapters, conglomerate diversification brings many advantages to the Overseas Chinese, yet it also saps families' resources and managerial talent. As we also profiled in the previous chapter, after the Asian crises, some Overseas Chinese companies, such as the CP Group, established procedures by which to trim their foray into diverse industries. The Thai conglomerate is in BCG's top 100; but the group is also an unspectacular contender in many industries, from telecoms to convenience stores, and is now moving into making automobiles. San Miguel of the Philippines, a big beer-and-food conglomerate, recently talked of trying its hand at generating electricity. Michael Porter once damningly summed up this dilettantism: "These companies don't have strategies; they do deals." Gerry Ambrose in Aberdeen Asset Management's Kuala

FIGURE 6.3: *Labor Productivity (Output) Per Employed Person*

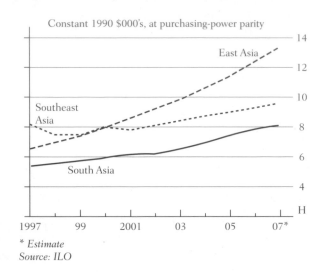

* *Estimate*
Source: ILO

Lumpur office also lamented the difficulty of finding Malaysian companies with "a business plan that will last 10 years." The avoidance of long-term strategic plans, and the tandem difficulty of investing in specific businesses for long-term gains, often arises because of succession fears in the Overseas Chinese companies.

Lack of professionalization

Prior to 1998, the Overseas Chinese companies displayed a lack of procedural controls, processes, and structures. The managers had within their personal memory models for successful management. Processes and procedures, policy statements, and defined structures did not exist. Corporate memories maintained no institutionalized knowledge; individuals' personal memory and unique experience captured all the company's knowledge.

Governance issues and improved IT have alleviated this problem in the post-crisis era; even so, it persists at the highest levels of Overseas Chinese companies. The best companies have highly professionalized management, with the CEO equally conversant in both traditional Chinese decision making and Western planning techniques. Nevertheless, *guanxi* remains the exclusive province of the CEO and immediate subordinates. As we discussed earlier, *guanxi* affords an advantage for rapid decision making and implementation of decisions; but it leaves most managers without the institutional knowledge they need when serious disruptions in key personnel occur. Perversely, the growing practice of having the CEOs' children prove themselves in other companies, though laudable, may worsen this problem. The heirs, now establishing their managerial mettle in other (frequently Western) companies, fail to forge their own relationships among the traditional business partners and associates of their family's companies.

Thanks to the cultural emphasis on seniority, some companies tend to favor senior employees over younger but better performers. This preference for seniority can significantly hinder Overseas Chinese companies from retaining promising, ambitious young managers. The tendency to honor senior staff and managers also causes problems for many companies that are trying to professionalize. The unwillingness to run counter to traditional values and seniority, manifested among many members of the Overseas Chinese companies' senior and middle managers, can cause significant tension and conflict during the professionalization process. Many Overseas Chinese companies have worked hard to change their company's traditional Chinese business culture, but as exemplified by Li & Fung, many continue to seek out managers who have a preference for traditional Chinese business cultures.

The next chapter discusses the implications of the Overseas Chinese style of management. It also proposes a strategic planning model for the future.

CHAPTER 7

Competitive Implications of the Overseas Chinese: Doing Business with the New Asian Emperors

> Why stop doing business and start playing golf? It's only another game.
>
> **—A member of Robert Kuok's family** explaining the 83-year-old tycoon's three failed retirement efforts

For our research, we have interviewed in depth the chairmen of the major Overseas Chinese companies, and many of their senior managers. The Appendix lists some of the CEOs and major Overseas Chinese executives we interviewed, although we also drew on our work with them over two decades and more. In our final chapter, we discuss the advantages and disadvantages of competing against or cooperating with the Overseas Chinese. Drawing on the lessons from the most competitive Overseas Chinese companies, we also present a roadmap for strategic success in Asia.

In the first three sections, we discuss the implications for practice of the Overseas Chinese management styles in regard to competing multinationals, regional governments, and researchers who study them. We close this book with a road map to chart a course for strategic success in Asia that draws on the best practices and insights offered by the New Asian Emperors.

General Implications for Multinationals

In Southeast and East Asia, multinationals serve markets about which there is little information and research. To compete success-fully, multinationals from the industrialized economies must off-set the competitive advantage that the Overseas Chinese have in knowledge, even if the multinationals seek local partners (Haley and Haley, 1997). The multinationals must determine which mar-kets they aim to serve. Even though information is lacking, it does exist for the multinationals; their managers must dredge it up, col-late and analyze it, and seek out both hard and subjective data, as well as the most up-to-date and historical data. Western managers must treat research as an investment that will produce substantial returns; they should remember that those returns come from both earning future profits and avoiding future losses.

The multinationals can use the data they gather to prioritize potential products and markets, and identify the major players and influences in them. They can determine which players would prove legitimate, beneficial partners and which they should avoid at all cost. Just as in the industrialized economies, managers will find some Overseas Chinese and other local companies that appear more desirable as partners than others. Some Overseas Chinese companies have larger networks or greater competencies in areas of business where the foreign companies appear most lacking; or they seem more trustworthy and upright than other partners. Previous, successful working relationships with other foreign companies are a good indication of the desirability of a local company. The multi-nationals' managers should use this information to move independ-ently into product markets, or make rapid decisions if a desirable partner approaches with an opportunity.

As we discussed in previous chapters, Overseas Chinese compa-nies exhibit great speed in decision making. Unlike Japanese firms, which sometimes seem to move glacially, the Overseas Chinese network companies move quickly and expect rapid decisions from their potential partners; multinationals following standard operating procedures will probably lose several good opportunities. To move rapidly, however, managers cannot wait until they perceive a potential opportunity to research a market; they must have the knowledge substantially on hand and, as Slywotzky and Shapiro (1993) said, "leverage to beat the odds."

To succeed in Asia, Western multinationals must develop a flexible corporate culture that can respond to diverse managerial cultures, promote cultural sensitivity, and seek out home/host similarities. Most often, Asian managers best manage Asian operations. Managers must have close links in each country to speed decision making and have ready access to the highest levels of corporate management. Using more locals with strong local connections and building trust-based relationships are two ways to establish stronger links to local information. However, if the multinationals cannot locate suitable locals, somewhere in the multinationals' management groups, there are people generally with backgrounds that have better prepared them to deal with the Asian environment than is normal for the company's managers. For example, Philips selected a highly trusted and historically successful Mexican executive from its Latin American operations, Reinaldo Wences, to become general manager of their regional headquarters in Singapore. Philips made this appointment on the premise that the Latin American environment, with its high uncertainty, poor information base, and highly personal autocratic style of management, would better prepare an executive for Asia than would working in their European headquarters; in this instance at least, the company appears to have made the right decision.

Multinationals operating in Asia should institute experience-based training programs and man Asian operations with line managers rather than people who have come up in staff functions. Line managers can better understand their senior counterparts at most

DUE DILIGENCE IN ASIA

The Tale of Sherlock Holmes vs.
The Informational Void

D UE DILIGENCE INVESTIGATION forms a thriving industry in Hong Kong. Potential business partners are investigated to ensure that they have a sound corporate history and can meet their side of an agreement or contract. U.S. companies constitute the biggest users of due-diligence advisors, usually in relation to prospective partners in China and Hong Kong, though Southeast Asia has assumed increasing importance. Such external advice can prove highly valuable to foreign companies, especially those operating in China, where poorly enforced business regulations may prevent recovery of losses from fraudulent or unsatisfactory partners. One prominent accounting firm has more than 300 full-time staff working in China on due diligence alone.

Due diligence can focus on either the company or a project, and can include review of articles of incorporation, bylaws, and other documentation to gauge governance structures; confirmation of registration with government authorities where required by local laws; checking of companies and individuals against lists of various violations published by a U.S. review of program reports to determine organizational experience, capabilities, and track records; assessment of organizational reputation before the local audience; review of financial information, including current and past budgets showing sources and uses of revenue; and review of internal or independent financial data when available.

Due diligence relies almost exclusively on hard data and publicly available information, especially as used in the Western and industrialized countries for strategic decisions. Due diligence often ignores the soft information that our research has shown assumes paramount importance for strategic success in Southeast Asia. Therefore, we argue that due diligence forms a necessary, through not sufficient, condition for business success in Southeast Asia.

Asian firms because they have had many of the same operational experiences. Line-management experience also helps top managers build local information links more rapidly; the senior Asian managers with which they interact should relate to line managers more as equals than they do with staff managers.

Finally, managers should learn to recognize the evolution of Asian relationships. Unlike many other networks around the world, an individual enjoys flexible acceptance within an Overseas Chinese network. Acceptance can vary with events over which the individual has no influence; the individual's acceptance does not depend solely on the individual's actions, but also on others that affect the situation(s) in which the individual interacts with the network. Western managers do not have total freedom to enact some behaviors that may help cement their position within an Overseas Chinese network. (This has nothing to do with bribery, but with freedom to act independently and involve their family in business relationships as completely as the Overseas Chinese often do.) Given this situation, Western managers must learn to recognize the cues given by the Overseas Chinese to indicate the state of a relationship between two people at any time.

Specific Implications for Multinationals

From our experience and research with foreign operations in Asia, we now offer specific recommendations for dealing with multinationals' strategic competitiveness, human resource practices, technology, contracts, distribution, promotion, and pricing.

Strategic competitiveness

The strong defensive positions of the Overseas Chinese

However aggressive the Overseas Chinese may seem because of their speed of strategy formulation and market implementation, they basically employ defensive strategies. Their strategies seek to generate profits through maintaining an environment that shields two of their core competencies: their decision-making style and their control of information in an informational void.

Without the informational void, Overseas Chinese companies could face severe challenges from nonnetwork, local firms and from foreign multinationals with competitive advantages in product and process technology, R&D, advertising and promotional skills, distribution, and finances. The informational void gives the Overseas Chinese companies the ability to compete with foreign multinationals by trading their contacts for the multinational's advantages. The informational void also reduces domestic competition for the Overseas Chinese by hindering the growth of nonnetwork businesses; these local, nonnetwork businesses would compete directly against the Overseas Chinese in the various product markets and would give foreign multinationals alternative local, Asian strategic partners.

Despite the basic truth of these statements, a decade after the financial crisis, significantly different nuances have emerged. The best Overseas Chinese companies have surfaced from the financial and SARS crises just as influential with local government authorities as before (Studwell, 2007), but with renewed emphasis on acquiring

Western-trained talent and the best continuing education and train-ing for managers and staff. Founder Tanoto of RGM emphasized this point when he told us, "The key is always constant learning; adapting to changing environments; it is continuous improvement." Similarly, Stephen Riady of Lippo Group told us, "We can no longer depend on *guanxi*. We need professional managers to run our businesses. The operations have become too big and too complex; so the move is to more and more separation between management and ownership. It is not complete yet, but it is well on its way."

The poor offensive positions of the Overseas Chinese

Unlike Japanese firms, few of the Overseas Chinese companies appear likely to develop a strong competitive position within the foreign multinationals' home market in the short run, barring sig-nificant investment in managerial personnel. The Overseas Chinese decision-making core competency becomes both their strength and their weakness. Until Overseas Chinese companies develop a core competency less dependent on their home environment, as the large Japanese and Korean firms did, they will fail as strong compet-itors outside the seemingly mazelike environment serving as their bastion. This weakness implies that foreign multinationals invest-ing in research, data acquisition, and contacts can attack Overseas Chinese competitors in their home market; conversely, the major-ity of Overseas Chinese companies will have difficulty retaliating against the multinationals in their own home market.

The Asian financial crisis has once again modified this situation among the best Overseas Chinese companies. Through Hutchison Whampoa, Li Ka-shing has expanded significantly beyond his Hong Kong base to control ports at both ends of the Panama Canal, four ports in Mexico, and cruise-ship terminals in Ecuador and Argentina. In the Bahamas, Li has been constructing the Freeport container port and cruise-ship terminal and the Grand Bahama Airport. He also controls Husky Oil, Canada's fifth largest corpo-ration, and is a technology leader in the race to develop shale-oil technology. Acer Computers of Taiwan has overtaken China's Lenovo Computers (purchaser of IBM's PC business) to entrench itself as the world's third-largest PC company. Li & Fung offers global supply-chain solutions to its clients through offices on all the continents save Australia and Antarctica. Many Overseas Chinese investors are preparing to enter U.S. real-estate markets between late 2009 and mid-2010, speculating that the U.S. markets will move strongly upward at that time.

Human resource practices

Rotation of staff for MNCs

The Overseas Chinese companies' core competencies (discussed in the previous chapter) also indicate that the practice at many foreign multinationals of rotating executives in foreign postings every two or three years proves counterproductive in fighting the competition.

First, rotation diminishes the multinationals' ability to employ emergent strategies in Asia. This effect occurs because the multinational managers often fall short of gaining intimate knowledge of the market; they cannot recognize the emerging patterns in the environment or in the company's local operations, and consequently they cannot generate effective, Asia-based emergent strategies.

Second, companies do not build contacts; humans do. When multinationals rotate employees out of Asian countries, they lose the employees' contacts. The damage may prove minimal in the short period of two or three years; an employee could not have had an opportunity to build a substantial number of influential contacts. However, if after three years, the multinational managers could socialize and interact with the local business communities effectively and build contacts, then the multinationals were probably only starting to get a substantial return from those managers.

Again, some post-crisis evolution has occurred. Some Asians view executives representing well-known and established companies as having characteristics that can be inferred from the reputation of the company for which they work—that is, a GE executive will have characteristics associated with GE, including a degree of trustworthiness. This evolution in Asian beliefs indicates that although executives representing well-known MNCs may be cut some slack until they prove their trustworthiness or lack of it, executives representing smaller, less-known companies have to work even harder to gain acceptance and build relationships for their company to compete effectively. One should remember, however, that Asians owe loyalty to individuals, and they view trust as something that individuals earn; many Asians do not perceive trust and loyalty as transferable. Incoming managers will not receive the benefits of goodwill that their predecessors accumulated during their time on the job, over and above the basic level of acceptance deriving from their company's overall perceived reputation. This becomes especially valid when relatively unknown multinationals choose to operate in Asia without local partners.

Staff's morale in the network

Historically, bright, nonfamily managers working for Overseas Chinese companies often wished they worked for someone else, thus creating an opportunity for multinationals to acquire experienced local executives. Surveys have historically shown that executives of local Hong Kong companies feel out of place and dissatisfied with their employment; most would prefer to work for companies where they could contribute to corporate strategy and aspire to top managerial positions (*Economist*, 1996).

This practice is changing in Asia's better companies. In all our interviews, both CEOs and their senior executives bragged about the pay scale their company offered; but they also indicated that many regional executives considered them employers of choice because they felt they could contribute to strategy formulation and success. Lim Siew Hua, chairwoman of Sateri International (of RGM Group), whom we interviewed, serves as a case in point. She served as Sateri's deputy chairwoman during the crisis and is highly influential in RGM's corporate hierarchy and in setting policy, and previously at Morgan Grenfell. Butt Lau of Li & Fung, Stephen Riady of Lippo Group, and Sukanto Tanoto and Lim of RGM all believed their company's pay scale is competitive with Western MNCs. They also touted their respective company as an employer of choice that does not lose employees to other companies. Riady made the point to us in this manner:

> We can no longer depend on *guanxi*. We need professional managers to run our businesses. The operations have become too big and too complex. . . . The important thing is to get good and trusted people, and then reward them correctly. The rewards must be appropriate—if you need good management, you must pay appropriately for the quality you want, and then you must make sure that the rewards provide the incentives appropriate to accomplish your desired goals.

However, many Overseas Chinese companies continue to buy manager loyalty through substantial annual performance bonuses and generous retirement schemes, practices that some Western companies also follow. Some very competitive and successful Overseas Chinese companies still refuse to match Western multinational pay scales. These companies, such as Hong Leong Group, depend on their human-resource department to find those special people who have excellent professional skills but who, as Kwek Leng Beng, executive chairman of the group, said, "prefer local companies like ours. We have manufacturing, hotels, properties, finance, and so on. They can move from one industry to another. We may not pay as well, but we do pay well and we work hard to find those top executives who fit into our culture and who prefer to not only live in our culture, but also to work in it."

Succession

Today, unlike the nepotistic image that many people still associate with the Overseas Chinese, well-run Overseas Chinese companies generally do not employ a large number of family members. Younger family members, even sons and daughters from the controlling family, have to find work at other companies. The companies hire the younger family members only after they have gained experience and proven themselves as capable managers.

When we asked him if his children worked for Hong Leong Group, Kwek Leng Beng said, "Right now no, they are working for others; they need to learn the hard way before they return. Even if they don't return, that would be fine." Wee Ee Cheong of United Overseas Bank explained the situation to us in this way: "UOB is a professionally managed bank, operating in a well-regulated industry with a robust governance framework. A significant proportion of our shareholder base is foreign institutions. We believe in ongoing transformation to stay relevant and competitive. We have to be doing so. At the end of the day, the Wee family is much more interested in growing shareholder value than in growing our control."

In company after company, we observed minimal family presence in management made up of only proven business professionals. Li & Fung has only Victor and William Fung, the two brothers who bought out the balance of their family. Acer's Stan Shih will not hire his children. Sukanto Tanoto of RGM has only a few family members on board in the company; the rest are professional managers. The new Overseas Chinese companies increasingly approximate professionally managed corporations that require similar economic justification for decisions, but with greater emphasis on line experience in strategic planning and decision making than most Western corporations.

Products and technology

Widespread lack of respect for intellectual property rights severely affects product management in Asia. Many attribute the problem to there being no rule of law. Indeed, the Indian government has openly used this argument in urging multinationals to invest in India rather than in other parts of Asia. The Indian government has also changed the basis for patents from process to product in the pharma and agro-chemical sectors, to synchronize with its other patent laws and to the preferences of the West's pharmaceutical industry. The truth continues to appear worse in many respects than the myths.

Intellectual property rights are a difficult issue when countries are striving to develop domestic manufacturing capacity. During the 18th and early 19th centuries, the fledgling U.S. government adopted policies of acquiring foreign technology, legally or illegally, and recruiting skilled foreign craftsmen (Heilbroner and Singer, 1984). Economically, developing nations have incentives to ignore intellectual property rights; the developing countries need the new technologies to move into higher value-added industries that industrialized nations control. As we indicated in an earlier chapter, in Confucian societies, intellectual property rights never existed historically. Lack of historical precedence reinforces the economic rationale for ignoring these rights and puts their protection in peril. To protect intellectual property rights effectively, a government must shift both violators and lower- and midlevel legal authorities from feeling unjustly persecuted by their enforcement. In many situations, local legal authorities ignore property right violations when there is minimal incentive to do so.

Additionally, Confucian societies have generally not enjoyed the rule of law in commercial transactions. Western-style commercial law did not evolve in Confucian cultures, which persecuted merchants. The present, sorely underdeveloped legal systems in many Asian countries have significant weaknesses in enforcing laws promulgated in more recent times. Also, the Confucian cultures' ethical structure, based on the context of established relationships, affects the ethical perception of intellectual property rights. Most intellectual property pirates have no relationship with the companies or individuals from which they steal; hence, they owe no ethical duty to those companies or individuals.

Finally, with reference to China, unlike the era of Mao's control, the present government does not rule with an iron fist throughout the country. The provincial governments' power vis-à-vis the central government's has increased significantly in recent years. This power shift has augmented the central government's difficulty in enforcing its laws and treaties without the provincial governments' strong support. In some instances, the provincial governments refuse to render this support. In many respects, the situation parallels the old imperial efforts to prevent Chinese traders from conducting overseas transactions. Central authorities passed their edicts and tried to enforce them, but merchant traders and their networks of local authorities frustrated the center's efforts.

Multinationals should move production as close to major markets as possible. However, the companies should also consider the differences between nations' legal statutes and "natural law" or national ethical perceptions. Natural laws have potency, and legal statutes often fail to overturn them in the short run. Currently, besides India, the major Asian economies most successful in protecting intellectual property rights are Singapore, the Philippines, and Thailand, with Malaysia making an increasingly successful effort.

Contract flexibility

Many Western businesspersons in Asia have problems with the seeming flexibility of contractual agreements in Asia. The Bundesbank's difficulty in collecting on some of its loans to Chinese companies, including government-owned firms, presents a classic example. When Chinese debtor companies ceased paying on loans, Bundesbank representatives demanded resumption of payment. Their Chinese counterparts responded by arguing that circumstances had changed, and hence the terms of the contract must change. Contractual flexibility follows Chinese custom.

We have recounted the story of the great Chinese trader Howqua, who paid for quicksilver at the new market price rather than the stated contract price after the price rose abruptly. In Howqua's case, Western businessmen profited from the custom. Few businesspersons of the present era would follow Howqua's example and freely pay a greater price than contracted. Given Confucian and Chinese custom, however, managers should not expect Chinese executives to forgo efforts to alter contractual terms to their benefit.

Contractual flexibility took hold among Chinese businesspersons because of the nature of their business. Business-to-business transactions occurred largely between long-time associates at the very least, if not actual family members. Hence, if circumstances changed abruptly in favor of one party to the transaction and to the substantial detriment of the other, they would renegotiate the contract so that neither party would suffer unbearably from changed circumstances. This consideration offered to one's trading partner stemmed from self-interest. An unhappy trading partner might not only refuse to do any further business with the offending individual, but also campaign against him within his network, or even offer evidence against him with imperial authorities.

Distribution

Many of the limitations of distributing goods through any developing nation's infrastructure apply to Southeast Asia. Thanks to their early and continuing dominance of most significant distributors, wholesale and retail, in the region, the Overseas Chinese companies created the same regional situation as the major commercial families did in Latin America. In 1996, K-Mart was forced to withdraw from Singapore after a costly attempt to break into the cutthroat, minimal-margin environment in a major Asian retailing center's mass market.

Trade was the original business of the Overseas Chinese. Despite the number of businesses the Overseas Chinese have entered into since, they have never entirely left the business of trade. Friends or long-established business relations supply most Overseas Chinese merchants, retailers, and wholesalers. For the larger merchant companies, suppliers include member companies of the same business group and network. Networks give local merchants tremendous competitive advantage when confronting outside competitors. In most Asian countries, discriminatory pricing is *not* an illegal practice.

Promotion and pricing

Asian culture affects promotion practices. Firms must seek to ensure they do not offend local custom and mores, and that they remain within the law. To some extent, most Asian cultures exhibit linguistic sensitivity; many Asian countries outlaw public signboards in foreign languages. Yet periodic crackdowns occur because of lax enforcement (especially in Indonesia and Vietnam). To operate successfully in the region, multinationals need local agencies to apprise them of local enforcement trends and protect their interests.

Western companies often face pricing difficulties because of the additional costs associated with international business operations. Additionally, when necessary, Overseas Chinese companies can accept very low margins because of their family control. The large Overseas Chinese companies can also frequently subsidize predatory pricing practices through conglomerate diversification. As mentioned just above, discriminatory pricing is not illegal in most Asian countries.

Implications for Regional Governments

Overseas Chinese managers may pare labor costs and middlemen through sourcing goods from connections abroad; however, they generally contribute much more significantly to the countries in which they operate (Haley and Haley, 1998). The Overseas Chinese companies intensify competition within indigenous industries, often forcing prices down to benefit consumers. Bulk buying, direct importing, and other traditional practices are examples of the New Asian Emperors' global connections translating to social and commercial benefits. The Overseas Chinese also facilitate global trade. Consequently, regional government policies should incorporate effective understanding of their companies' economic and developmental importance.

First, for regional governments, the Overseas Chinese family companies contribute to economic viability, especially in an economic crisis. For example, as we noted previously, Thailand, like most regional economies dominated by the Overseas Chinese, rebounded substantially after the 1997 financial crisis. Through traditional business practices such as keeping assets liquid, lowering borrowing, and demonstrating strategic flexibility and speed, the Overseas Chinese have generally survived Thailand's 1997 financial crisis and helped to rebuild the country's economy (Vatikiotis and Daorueng, 1998).

Second, for effective governance regional governments often have to confront and should quell local hostility toward the Overseas Chinese. In Indonesia, the country's visible Overseas Chinese have encountered local animosity since colonial times. But the 1997 economic crisis brought about fresh, intense waves of Overseas Chinese bashing. Indonesia's wealthiest Overseas Chinese have long had escape pods for their families and businesses such as foreign homes, foreign passports, and overseas bank accounts; however, the tensions that arose after the 1997 crisis forced even the middle class to consider flight—and some did. In 1998, the Overseas Chinese middle class triggered an outflow from Indonesia of at least US$1 billion in capital and probably much more (Gilley, McBeth, Dolven, and Tripathi, 1998). Overseas Chinese pullouts could have heightened economic distress and stepped up ethnic violence; however, the long-term implications might have been more worrying if the Overseas Chinese departures had hollowed out corporate Indonesia. Wilson Nababan, president of the credit-analysis firm CISI Raya Utama in Jakarta, reflected on the issue at the time when he said, "We need Chinese businesses to attract foreign investment. We should be encouraging them to stay, not chasing them away" (quoted in Gilley, McBeth, Dolven, and Tripathi, 1998, p. 47). More important, Indonesia could have lost a well-educated group valued for its entrepreneurial savvy and managerial abilities. Fortunately, this did not happen.

The Overseas Chinese stayed in post-crisis Indonesia and fought to save their fortune and the Indonesian economy. Sukanto Tanoto described his fight to save RGM when he told us:

> In 1997, I was in the middle of a US$2 billion expansion when the crisis hit. We were really hurt. President Suharto resigned in 1998 and foreign investors feared civil war. The original funding plan collapsed—the local banks collapsed; the foreign banks walked away. Cash was king. I had to sell my assets in China. From 1998 to 2000, I brought about US$1 billion into Indonesia to invest in my projects here. Without that money, I would have no business today. Now to be clear, not everyone jumped ship. I still had the support of many foreign investors, but the big banks left. If I had been forced to sell at that time, I would not have gotten 50 cents on the dollar.

RGM had company. The Salim Group, which prior to the 1997 crisis was the largest of all Overseas Chinese companies in Southeast Asia, was especially hard hit.

Some governments are actively trying to take advantage of the Overseas Chinese network capabilities. As mentioned in a previous chapter, the government of Singapore, for instance, began a Website, the World Chinese Business Network, to stimulate further foreign investment in Singapore and increase value-added production in the Island State. In the post-crisis decade, the government renamed and repositioned the site as the Cyber Business Network to focus on improving access to technology for companies operating in the City State. The site lists Overseas Chinese companies and networks operating in Singapore to facilitate potential foreign collaborators' contacts with Overseas Chinese companies.

ANTHONY SALIM

Reinventing the Empire

A NTHONY SALIM HEADS INDOFOOD Sukses Makmur, probably the world's largest instant-noodle manu- facturer. Salim is trying to change the Salim Group, which was until the Asian financial crisis of 1998 Indonesia's largest private company and one of Asia's most influential and sprawling Overseas Chinese groups. At the apex, Salim con- trolled Indonesia's largest retail bank and largest cement plant, and one of the world's biggest flour mills. The Salim Group also engaged in car manufacturing, television broadcasting, petrochemicals, textiles, construction, and other businesses.

When the economic crisis hit Indonesia in 1997–1998, Salim lost his shirt as well as his chief patron, President Suharto. Salim and his family, including the patriarch, Liem Sioe Liong, fled to Singapore as angry mobs burned their prop- erty. With its close ties to Suharto, Salim Group emerged as a favorite target for the former president's enemies. Subsequent governments frequently sought to prove their independence from Suharto by getting tough with Salim. The group emerged from the 1997 crisis much reduced; on December 14, 1998, the Indonesian Bank Restructuring Agency (IBRA) forced Salim to surrender control of 107 Salim Group companies to PT Holdiko Perkasa, a special company it had established to receive, manage, and sell the Salim Group's assets. Throughout 1998–2000, the Indonesian government pressured several of the group's foreign partners to recant on or change agreements they had negotiated with Anthony Salim (Dieleman, 2007).

Once the storm subsided, Anthony Salim set out to rebuild his shattered empire. It took him nearly five years to restructure the group, shedding lucrative assets such as Bank Central Asia and settling debts of 52 trillion rupiah (about $5.8 billion) with the Indonesian authorities. He retained control of Indofood through the First Pacific Company, a Salim-controlled investment and management company listed in Hong Kong. Despite these tough years, and debt, Indofood's business grew. Indofood's balance sheet appears reasonably healthy today, according to investment analysts.

To help him piece the empire back together, Salim sought to shore up his reputation as a good manager. In June 2004, he won appointment as the chief executive of Indofood, replacing a high-profile professional, Eva Hutapea. "To most bankers, Salim Group's reputation is much better than other conglomerates', and they are willing to lend," said Lim Chei Wei, an independent corporate analyst in Jakarta who has been strongly critical of some groups owned by Indonesian Chinese. "I have to admit that the Salims actually know how to build a business and create value" (Vatikiotis, 2004, C-4).

Salim's ideas include exploiting Southeast Asia's expanding web of free trade; putting people and companies in place in Malaysia, Thailand, Singapore, and Vietnam; and following with Indofood's products. Indofood currently gets 10 percent of its revenue from exports but is aiming to increase that to 20 percent. Some analysts applaud Salim's strategy; Indofood has an advantage over many Chinese noodle companies because it has learned to make flavors that cater to different regional tastes.

But critics still question if Salim can transform Indofood into an integrated regional food giant like Thailand's Charoen Pokphand. Salim's lack of political patronage and also the pyramidal control that he exercises over about 400 companies worries some stakeholders. In an increasingly open Indonesian market, multinationals such as Unilever and Wings (the latter an Indonesian Chinese family-owned company new to the noodle market) are giving Indofood a run for its money. These criticisms do not appear to deter Salim. "We are a major food company," he said. "There is no limit to how we can grow" (Vatikiotis, 2004, C-4).

SINGAPORE'S ECONOMIC DEVELOPMENT BOARD

Network Facilitator

THE ECONOMIC DEVELOPMENT BOARD (EDB) of Singapore serves as the Singapore government's main mechanism to encourage development of Singapore's "external wing." The EDB was created in 1961 with the primary role of attracting foreign capital to Singapore. This role has now shifted significantly to promoting Singaporean investment abroad, and to this end, it has offices around the world.

The EDB does not advise Singaporean companies where to invest but assists in negotiating with foreign governments and governmental authorities. If Singaporean companies intend to invest in China, for example, the EDB can assist in negotiations with the relevant provincial governments or with the government in Beijing; but the EDB leaves dealings with the municipal governments to the companies themselves. The

EDB leaves advice on where to invest to private consultants. The EDB supplies this assistance only if convinced that positive benefits will flow to other Singaporean companies.

The EDB also acts as a catalyst for consortia. Singapore-based companies can approach the EDB for assistance in locating suitable partners for projects. The EDB then attempts to locate such partners, either from within Singapore or from overseas. Occasionally, the EDB identifies opportunities and then alerts suitable companies to exploit them. The EDB does not charge for its services as network facilitator.

Implications for Researchers

We have noted the need for researchers to develop theories that reflect the Overseas Chinese business groups' decision-making and cultural styles. Before the crises, too much of businesspersons' and researchers' understanding of the Overseas Chinese and their network structures constituted a Western interpretation of their activities—without consideration of cultural or historical origins. To a great extent, this remains true. Many researchers studying Chinese business strategy continue to base their expectations and assumptions on understanding of Western companies, using surveys of middle managers, for example, to extrapolate on strategic decision making (for examples, see Chen, 2001; Lee and Phan, 2006; Fan and Phan, 2007). Strategic decisions in any company originate at the top ranks of management, and this approach of convenience and accessibility poses problems for our more complex understanding of Western companies as well. However, when studying Chinese and Overseas Chinese companies, these researchers' assumptions and expectations generate misleading conclusions. In Chinese companies, strategic management falls under senior managers' exclusive purview; indeed, many middle managers would consider discussing their company's strategic plans with outsiders an unethical practice. Overseas Chinese and Chinese middle managers also consider control of information and knowledge as a major source of competitive advantage. Consequently, they are unlikely to convey accurate or vital information to researchers.

Overseas Chinese networks differ significantly from U.S. business networks. Asian networks show much more resilience than do the individual firms that make up the networks (Redding, 1996). U.S. business networks appear relatively weak and generally represent the individual firm's short-term institutional interests (Mizruchi and Schwartz, 1987). Many network theorists view networks as something that managers can manipulate for the company's sole benefit (Charan, 1991) without recognizing that networks arise and exist for the benefit of all involved parties. Through an institutional perspective, the Asian economies appear network-based whereas the U.S. economy appears firm-based. Overseas Chinese networks seem normative, relational, hierarchical, and substantive, just as Confucianism would require them to be. We have argued that future researchers should enquire and elaborate on these characteristics to develop useful theories of the networks. These new theories would then better explain both Asian and Western networking behaviors and systems, and develop best-practice behaviors for promotion of effective cooperation between the two systems. Haley, Haley, and Tan (2004) have made one such attempt. If, as Fei (1992) and Hamilton and Zheng (1992) argued, civilizational rather than cultural differences distinguish the East and West, the implications for international business competition have been inadequately explored.

Second, researchers should enquire more specifically into how the Overseas Chinese and their networks shape industrial and financial institutions and structures. Many Asian developing countries' economic hierarchies arise from the networks that control so much of these economies (Haley and Haley, 1997). Consequently, to understand and predict market evolution and development, researchers must more fully comprehend the Overseas Chinese networks' institutional and developmental roles in these markets. Some research into this area has already begun (see Chang, 2006).

Speculations About the Future

When Nakamura (1992) stated that the strategic-management processes of the newly industrializing countries of East and Southeast Asia were following the same pattern as Japan's, he was arguing that the future of Asian business approximated Japan's history. This understanding is fallacious. For various reasons, some that we mentioned in earlier chapters, the future of the Overseas Chinese and their business structures and strategies in Southeast and East Asia appears likely to follow an independent course, and will interact with Western practice and behavior in their unique ways. Managers and policymakers must determine an independent course because of the market's size, and also because of potential influences on business practices globally.

Many believe that the reforms the Asian governments are undertaking today will make the Asian economies resemble the U.S. economy (Kristof, 1998). This belief follows the theory that the regulatory environment will shape business structures and competitive practice. We can also speculate on future directions by considering present-day events and trends: for example, many of the Overseas Chinese companies' heirs hold positions of authority within their family company. What role do they play? How do they see their future evolving? The second generation of Kuoks—Robert Kuok's sons Beau Kuok Khoon Chen and Kuok Khoon Ean (also known as Ean Kuok), as well as nephews Chye Kuok Khoon Ho and Edward Kuok Khoon Loong and niece Kay Kuok Oon Kwong, all play key roles in his companies. Second-generation managers from the Overseas Chinese business groups have perceptions of their roles in their companies and societies, and some were willing to share their perceptions with us for this book.

The first generation of Overseas Chinese business founders took what they best could use of Confucian philosophy and discarded what they found less desirable or useful. In an earlier chapter, we noted the lack of primogeniture in Chinese culture, which has significantly deterred creation and maintenance of capital among Chinese families over the centuries. This first generation of the New Asian Emperors has largely sloughed off that burden on their fortunes. They are restructuring, reorganizing, and expanding their best-run companies to where they can compete globally. Li Ka-shing has consolidated his diversified and far-flung holdings into a more focused business empire.

At Wuthelam Group, the founder, Goh Cheng Liang, brought his son, Goh Hup Jin, back into the family business. At first blush, this practice may seem like business as usual; but Hup Jin earned an MBA in the United States and worked in major U.S. companies. When he returned home, his duties included helping to professionalize the company's management structure to take the company public. Goh Hup Jin and a cadre of professionals whom he brought into the business have professionalized management without excessively disrupting operations. To facilitate the transition, the company founded a subsidiary where skilled managers of the old school who could not adjust to the professionalization of management procedures and structures could move. These business practices exemplify the Confucian emphasis on personal loyalty, but also indicate good management.

We asked Goh Hup Jin what he felt made the management of the Overseas Chinese unique; he answered that Overseas Chinese business practices did not differ from Western practices strategically but rather only operationally. From his vantage point, he saw no changes in the future that would affect significantly the Overseas Chinese strategy of business; changes would primarily come in control and reporting processes owing to the continued growth of the company.

We also discussed future changes in strategic processes with Wee Cho Yaw, chairman of United Overseas Bank, and his son and heir, Wee Ee Cheong. As they described their strategic decision-making styles, little difference emerged between the two. For example, Wee Ee Cheong told us, "I don't let figures alone influence my decision. . . . They are used to confirm the decision rather than to arrive at the decision." Similarly, Wee Cho Yaw indicated to us, "How a good businessman reads the ups and downs of a market is often more valuable than statistics." Interestingly, both generations of managers felt that professional managers seemed too timid at times in their decision making and tended to make too many unwarranted assumptions and calculations about the markets.

In many instances, when we spoke with both senior traditional managers and their younger and more-educated heirs, we noticed remarkable similarity in their viewpoints and perspectives. The results of our interviews, research, work, and, yes, socializing with the New Asian Emperors indicated that lower and middle management in Overseas Chinese companies appear to be professionalizing; yet top-level management continues to strategize and manage largely drawing on their intimate knowledge of the business, its people, and the market. Their strategic style will continue to focus on and emphasize the senior managers' judgment and character, and not the numbers. Overseas Chinese management seems headed toward a combination of Western management procedures and processes at lower and middle levels of management; it continues to rely on the traditional Overseas Chinese management practices in higher levels of management. Other researchers have corroborated these observations (see Chan and Chiang, 1994).

Indeed, some of the New Asian Emperors appear to take their superstitions as seriously as their numbers. Li Ka-shing's watch runs exactly eight minutes fast, because *baat*, the Cantonese word for eight, is a homonym for *faat*, the Cantonese word for wealth. On the roof of the nondescript China Building in Central Hong Kong from where Li runs his empire, two 18th century cannons point to the Entertainment Building across the street from his office. These cannons serve to deflect the bad *fengshui* elements emanating from the other block. We should also not forget one of the second generation's managers, Manuel V. Pangilinan, of Hong Kong's First Pacific Group. In 1995, when First Pacific was preparing for what eventually became a US$1.6 billion bid for commercial property in Manila, he altered the original bid after his company's geomancer indicated that the bid did not constitute a propitious figure. "I did not want to tempt fate," Manuel Pangilinan argued; he raised his bid, unnecessarily as circumstances later revealed (*BusinessWeek*, September 2, 1996). Pangilinan outbid his closest competitor by some US$400 million; he would have won the bid even with his lower, unpropitious figure.

As we expanded our research to Greater China (Haley, Haley, and Tan, 2004), we continued to develop further our views on the future of Chinese management processes. In our book *The Chinese Tao of Business: The Logic of Successful Business Strategy* (2004), we proposed the Adaptive-Action Road Map (ARM). We will close this book with a discussion of how the management of Overseas Chinese companies has evolved over the past decade as the community struggled to overcome two serious crises.

The Adaptive-Action Road Map

We have argued in our analysis that both Western and Chinese management would converge into a basic model resembling the Adaptive-Action Road Map (ARM). The historical evolution of Western and Japanese management systems reveals that the U.S. arose to challenge the established economic powers of Europe, and then Japan arose to challenge those of Europe and the U.S. Rather than one-way transfer of knowledge and practice, the established and emerging economic powers' business cultures learned from

THE ADAPTIVE-ACTION ROAD MAP

The Road of Knowledge

Experiential, qualitative, and quantitative knowledge coalesce into a necessary whole for managers. The Road of Knowledge emphasizes that knowledge constitutes a strategic investment for companies. To take timely and necessary tactical and strategic actions, management must dedicate itself to acquiring and disseminating holistic knowledge.

The Road of Speed

Both strategic and tactical decision makers should use their knowledge of their company's businesses and markets to get their products to market before their competitors. For tactics, speed assumes paramount importance; speed requires that line managers at decision points have the authority to choose quickly from various options and beat competitors to the draw.

The Road of Action

The rapidity of change in emerging markets compounds difficulties in making product-market decisions. Uncertainty can slow action to a crawl. Most efforts to reduce uncertainty before taking action merely disguise uncertainty, not reduce it. The Road of Action irrevocably reduces uncertainty and allows managers to use market activities to learn more about product markets.

The Road of Results

Capital, time, effort, and personnel must flow toward success. The preliminary returns trickling in from various investments offer data on the investments' relative success. Managers should use these preliminary data to decide on further investments. Counterintuitively, short-term measures are often better indicators of success than long-term measures.

The Road of Relationships

People hold the key to success; successful companies encapsulate and focus people's collective action to create prosperity and customer value. Companies create value through formal and informal relationship networks. The Road of Relationships fuses relationship marketing and employee empowerment beyond commonly accepted views in the East and the West; Easterners generally apply the concepts only to long-time, close business associates, customers, and employees, but Westerners generally see the concepts as distinct and not conjoined.

The Road of Quality

Growing globalization and efficiencies are driving down costs; competitiveness will focus on quality and should know few limits. Because of this intense global competition, companies need both brand image and market presence, backed by quality, to best their competitors.

The Road of Passion

Managers should work as if their life depended on it; it does. The Road of Passion reflects the Eastern belief that executives should derive passionate joy from the industry in which they work, the Western belief that companies should passionately commit to the markets they serve, and the universal belief that executives should passionately dedicate efforts to their own and their company's success.

The Road of Legacy

Management shapes perceptions and eventually legacies. Managers should display a commitment to leaving their society and the world a better place than they found it, to bringing something special into the world. Companies that act responsibly while generating profits will also reap long-term success.

Source: Haley, Haley, and Tan (2004).

one another, adopted each other's best practices, and adapted techniques to exploit their own strengths as they took action to compete successfully. Our model for success consists of eight roads to success, represented graphically in Figure 7.1.

FIGURE 7.1: *The Adaptive-Action Road Map*

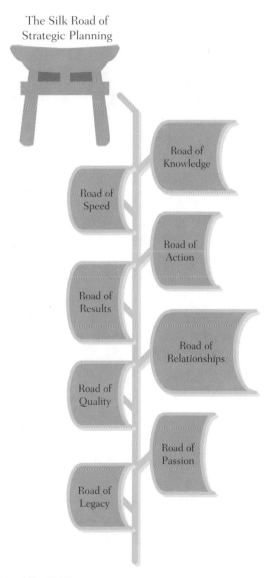

The Silk Road of
Strategic Planning

Road of
Knowledge

Road of
Speed

Road of
Action

Road of
Results

Road of
Relationships

Road of
Quality

Road of
Passion

Road of
Legacy

Source: Haley, Haley, and Tan (2004).

The ARM is basically an argument that East will meet West. Our research and interviews with Overseas Chinese and Western senior managers shed some light on the roads in the ARM and the manner in which Chinese and Western business executives are moving toward one another's practices.

The road of knowledge

Li & Fung views knowledge as so important that, like many successful Western multinationals, the company has started a full-time training and education center, the World Training Center. Victor Fung explained the effort to us this way: "We need the World Training Center to train the next generation of leaders. We do not need money to fund growth nearly as badly as we need trained, knowledgeable people to fund our growth."

Likewise, in explaining the rise of RGM in Indonesia, Sukanto Tanoto stated that "the key is always constant learning; adapting to changing environments and continuously improving." This theme pervaded all the interviews we conducted. In a more general emphasis on knowledge, Li Ka-shing of Hutchison Whampoa makes substantial contributions to universities, especially for medical programs. His contributions include about 70 percent of the annual budget of Shantou University in China, a university he helped to found (Haley, Haley, and Tan, 2004); and the founding of the Cheung Kong Graduate School of Business in Beijing.

Similar efforts from companies have arisen in the West. Well-known efforts such as GE's training program, and many others, ensure that companies can access a knowledgeable work force. For example, Sam Bergami, CEO and chair of Connecticut-based Alinabal Corporation, told us that he has worked with local universities for the past two decades to ensure that their engineering and business curricula reflect business, and specifically U.S. manufacturers' needs. Similarly, Arnold Alderman, founder and president of Anagenesis, Inc., noted the dwindling number of international business programs at U.S. universities. He told us that he has begun lobbying and collaborating with U.S. universities to ensure that they train their students in international business and cross-cultural issues. Outside the U.S., as the *grupo's* CEOs including Lorenzo Zanbrano, CEO of CEMEX, informed us, companies in Mexico have the practice of matching the compensation paid by the Instituto Tecnologico y de Estudios Superiores (ITESM) to any of its executives or engineers who agree to teach classes at the university. The road of knowledge appears to be converging for Overseas Chinese and Western managers.

The road of speed

Speed has always amounted to a competitive advantage for Overseas Chinese businesses. However, in the West, managers have not always viewed speed of decision making as an important strategic consideration. This appears to be changing. On March 27, 2006, *BusinessWeek* ran a cover story on "Speed Demons," or speed in decision making and implementing business strategies, especially in product development. Both Lorenzo Zambrano, CEO of CEMEX, and Rick Schart, JC Penney's vice president of transportation, emphasized the importance of speed for their companies. Zambrano explained how CEMEX's speed of decision making and implementation of decisions was crucial to offsetting the size advantage held by his two larger European competitors (CEMEX is the third largest cement maker in the world); Schart told us in 2008 that his company was implementing speed as a primary strategy. He said that although it once took 53 weeks to take a product from a fashion concept to floor displays, JC Penney reduced the time to 37 weeks and held 17 weeks as its goal—and was confident of achieving it.

The road of action

As we described earlier, the Overseas Chinese have always emphasized action. Some evidence indicates that researchers and managers in the West have also started considering it. Management theorist Clayton Christensen states, "By the time data shows that market share is eroding, it's often too late to fix the problem. . . . To make accurate predictions about where business is going, managers have to go on gut. When innovations are looming, what's worked in the past is a dangerous guide" (*Business* 2.0, 2002). Christensen presented an argument for action by stating that collecting all the desirable data will delay action intolerably, and in today's fast-paced environment, this may actually mislead; today, to predict accurately where their business is going, managers must "go on gut."

The road of results

Western companies have long emphasized the bottom line; some Overseas Chinese companies are increasingly doing so. As Justin Chiu of Cheung Kong Holdings told us, "In Cheung Kong, the basic issue is to bring results. You have an idea and implement it; so long as you get results all is well. That is the difference between Cheung Kong and the other companies. In the other companies, you may have an idea and implement it, but you do not get the chance to bring in results."

Every senior Overseas Chinese executive we interviewed echoed this sentiment. The best Overseas Chinese companies are emphasizing results and the bottom line. They are also refusing to carry dead weight just because it represents family members or their families' heritage devoid of tangible benefits.

The road of relationships

Both Western and Eastern business cultures emphasize relationships. However, the Overseas Chinese view relationships as personal and between individuals. Westerners view personal relationships as facilitating business, not as the dominant factor in business. Yet Western managers are perceiving the importance of myriad relationships, including those between companies and end users, which though not relationship marketing, can cement a company's competitive advantage through its stakeholders. Our research shows that the Overseas Chinese companies are converging on the Western side of this road by incorporating Western perspectives on end-user relationships. Even so, there is less evidence that Western companies are moving toward the Overseas Chinese side of the road.

Chiu of Cheung Kong Holdings spoke of this convergence to us. The SARS crisis hit Cheung Kong's real-estate market especially hard. A major development in Singapore, Costa Del Sol, faced a market that had suffered a 20 percent drop in property value. In discussing the company's response, Chiu told us:

> We had already sold to some 250 buyers prior to the crisis. When the crisis hit and the bottom dropped out of the market, we could not drop the price to meet the market. If we had, we would have angered the invested buyers. We had to hold the line on prices until the market came back to protect the buyers and our reputation for developments that were sound investments. In Cheung Kong, our culture is to work. In good years, we work hard. In bad years, we work harder.

RGM Sateri International's Lim Siew Hua brought up relationships with employees when she discussed the 1997 financial crisis with us. She said, "We had to manage on a cash-flow basis; profits became secondary to cash. The key was to live within our means and to prioritize payments. Employees' salaries ranked ahead of other payments." RGM sold its Chinese assets and repatriated the cash to complete its projects in Indonesia.

The road of quality

The road of quality has assumed increasing importance in the West and in Asia's low-cost emerging markets. In the West, and in the more economically developed emerging markets, high quality can offset the emerging-market companies' cost-based advantages. For emerging-market companies, quality satisfies the home country's growing middle class. An emphasis on quality also contributes to these companies' long-term economic viability by moving them up the value-added chain to establish an independent brand as costs rise.

Traditionally, rather than emphasizing the building of brand equity and product quality as primary competitive strategies, the Overseas Chinese emphasized control of distribution within geographic markets (Haley, Tan, and Haley, 1998). However, times have changed customs. As Chiu explained to us, at Cheung Kong "there is an emphasis on the backbone departments. There are three of these: human resources, internal auditing, and quality control. The backbone departments support the entire organization."

The road of passion

Passion has served as a key element in Overseas Chinese management. Goh Hup Jin of Wuthelam Group described to us the traditional decision making of the Overseas Chinese: he attributed successful decisions by executives to their working in industries that engendered a "labor of love" from them.

A steady stream of research has drawn correlations between passion and profitability (Buckingham and Coffman, 1999; Gubman, 2003, 2004). Once again, substantial convergence appears between Overseas Chinese and Western management. The most successful Overseas Chinese executives' passion for and deep involvement in their business also leads simultaneously to a seemingly detached attitude, similar to an athlete performing "in the zone." Indeed, many Chinese executives, including Li Ka-shing and Robert Kuok, have likened their involvement in their business to playing a game of golf—a pastime for which they also have passion.

The road of legacy

Legacy includes an executive's urge to leave behind a remembrance, such as a profitable, prominent company or a substantial contribution to charitable institutions that confer societal benefits. Both the Overseas Chinese and Western businesspersons have long desired to leave companies that create greater societal benefits than the norm. Examples of such companies abound: DuPont, General Motors, General Electric, Microsoft, Apple, and IBM are Western companies that fill the bill. Fewer Overseas Chinese companies exhibit legacy, primarily because they have a much shorter history than Western companies. However, among the Overseas Chinese companies, Acer, Cheung Kong Holdings, CP Group, Formosa Plastics, and a host of others aspire to legacy.

In many Western countries, prominent and wealthy businessper sons often contribute substantial fortunes to charitable causes. The best known might be the Carnegie Foundation, the Ford Foundation, the John D. Rockefeller Foundation, and the Gates Foundation. Many businesspersons in the West have made substantial contributions to universities and other educational institutions. Among the Overseas Chinese, such broad and deep charitable efforts are difficult to discern. One historical reason is the relative recency of foundations. The practice of creating and supporting great charitable foundations also seems most prevalent among historically wealthy societies, such as those in the West. Sociocultural reasons also explain charitable trends among the Overseas Chinese. Charitable contributions from Overseas Chinese appear primarily community-based, not societal as in the West; the contributions generally go to relatively closed subgroups within society, and outsiders thus have difficulty spotting them.

Akamatsu, K. (1998), "A Historical Pattern of Growth in Developing Countries," in Smitka, M. (ed.), *Japanese Pre-War Growth: Lessons for Development Theories?* London: Taylor & Francis.

Asiamoney (November 1994), Interview, p. 47.

Asian Development Bank (2003), "Assessing the Impact and Cost of SARS in Developing Asia," *Asian Development Outlook 2003 Update*.

Ayres, I. (2007), *Super Crunchers: Why Thinking-by-the-Numbers Is the New Way to Be Smart*, London: Bantam Press.

Balfour, F. (July 10, 2000), "Return of a Hong Kong Highflier (Int'l Edition)," *BusinessWeek Online*.

Buckingham, M., and C. Coffman (1999), *First, Break All the Rules: What the World's Greatest Managers Do Differently*, New York: Simon & Schuster.

Business 2.0 (August 2002), "What Makes a Great Leader?" pp. 72–75.

Campbell, J. (2004), *Institutional Change and Globalization*, Princeton, NJ: Princeton University Press.

Chan, K. B., and C. Chiang (1994), *Stepping Out: The Making of Chinese Entrepreneurs*, Singapore: Prentice Hall.

Chang, S. J. (2006), *Business Groups in East Asia*, Oxford, UK: Oxford University Press.

Charan, R. (September–October 1991), "How Networks Reshape Organizations—for Results," *Harvard Business Review*, reprint no. 91503.

Chen, M. J. (2001), *Inside Chinese Business*, Boston, MA: Harvard University Press.

Chu, T. C., and T. MacMurray (1993), "The Road Ahead for Asia's Leading Conglomerates," *McKinsey Quarterly*, #3, pp. 117–126.

Chung, C.-N., and I. P. Mahmood (2006), "*Taiwanese Business Groups: Steady Growth in Institutional Transition*," in S.-J. Chang (ed.), *Business Groups in East Asia: Financial Crisis, Restructuring and New Growth*, New York: Oxford University Press, pp. 70–93.

Claessens, S., S. Djankov, and L.H.P. Lang (2000), "Who Controls East Asian Corporations?" Financial Economics Unit, Financial Sector Practice Department, World Bank.

De Vienne, M.-S. (2004), "For a Tentative Modelization of the Economic Weight of Overseas Chinese at the Beginning of the 3rd Millennium." ISSCO V, May 10–14, Copenhagen.

Dieleman, M. (2007), *The Rhythm of Strategy: A Corporate Biography of the Salim Group of Indonesia*, Amsterdam, Netherlands: Amsterdam University Press.

East Asia Analytical Unit (1995), *Overseas Chinese Business Networks*, Canberra, Australia: AGPS Press, Department of Foreign Affairs and Trade.

Fan, T., and P. Phan (2007), "International New Ventures: Revisiting the Influences Behind the 'Born-Global' Firm," *Journal of International Business Studies*, Vol. 38, pp. 1113–1131.

Fei, X. (1992), *From the Soil: The Foundation of Chinese Society*, Berkeley: University of California Press.

Fernandez-Armesto, F. (1995), *Millennium*, London: Bantam Press.

Foucault, M. (1980), *Power/Knowledge: Selected Interviews and Other Writings*, 1972–1977, New York: Pantheon Books.

Friedland, J. (February 7, 1991), "Kuok: The Kingpin," *Far Eastern Economic Review*.

Fukuyama, F. (1995), *Trust: The Social Virtues and the Creation of Prosperity*, London: Penguin Books.

Ghosh, B. C., and C. O. Chan (1994), "A Study of Strategic Planning Behavior Among Emergent Businesses in Singapore and Malaysia," *International Journal of Management*, Vol. 11(2), pp. 697–706.

Gilley, B., J. McBeth, B. Dolven, and S. Tripathi (May 19, 1998), "Ready, Set . . .," *Far Eastern Economic Review*, pp. 46–50.

Granovetter, M. (2005), "Business Groups and Social Organization." In N. Smelser and R. Swedberg (eds.), *Handbook of Economic Sociology* (pp. 429–450), Princeton, NJ: Princeton University Press.

Gubman, E. (2003), *The Engaging Leader*. Chicago. Dearborn Press.

Gubman, E. (2004), "From Engagement to Passion for Work: The Search for the Missing Person," *Human Resource Planning*, 27(3), pp. 42–46.

Haley, G. T. (1997a), "A Strategic Perspective on Overseas Chinese Networks' Decision-Making," *Management Decision*, Vol. 35(8), pp. 587–594.

Haley, G. T. (December 24, 1997b), "The Values Asia Needs," *Business Times* (Singapore), Editorial and Opinion Section, p. 6.

Haley, G. T., and U. C. V. Haley (1997), "Making Strategic Business Decisions in South and Southeast Asia," Conference Proceedings of the First International Conference on Operations and Quantitative Management, Jaipur, India, Vol. II, pp. 597–604.

Haley, G. T., and U. C. V. Haley (1998), "Boxing with Shadows: Competing Effectively with the Overseas Chinese and Overseas Indian Networks in the Asian Arena," *Journal of Organizational Change Management*, Vol. 11(4), pp. 301–320.

Haley, G. T., and U. C. V. Haley (1999), "Managing Effectively in Southeast and East Asia," *General Management Review*, "A Special Compilation by the Indian Institute of Management, Calcutta", Vol. 1(1), pp. 37–46.

Haley, G. T., U. C. V. Haley, and C. T. Tan (2004), *The Chinese Tao of Business: The Logic of Successful Business Strategy*, John Wiley & Sons, Singapore and New York.

Haley, G. T., and C. T. Tan (1996), "The Black Hole of Southeast Asia: Strategic Decision-Making in an Informational Void," *Management Decision*, Vol. 34(9), pp. 43–55.

Haley, G. T., and C. T. Tan (1998), "East Versus West: Strategic Marketing Management Meets the Asian Networks," *Journal of*

Business & Industrial Marketing, Special Issue on "Business-to-Business Marketing in Asia."

Haley, G. T., C. T. Tan, and U. C. V. Haley (1998), *New Asian Emperors: The Overseas Chinese, Their Strategies and Competitive Advantages*, Butterworth-Heinemann, Singapore and Oxford, UK.

Haley, U. C. V. (1997), "The Myers-Briggs Type Indicator and Decision-Making Styles: Identifying and Managing Cognitive Trails in Strategic Decision Making," in C. Fitzgerald and L. Kirby (eds.), *Developing Leaders: Research and Applications in Psychological Type and Leadership Development*, Palo Alto, CA: Consulting Psychologists Press, pp. 187–223.

Haley, U. C. V., L. Low, and M. H. Toh (1996), "Singapore Incorporated: Reinterpreting Singapore's Business Environments Through a Corporate Metaphor." *Management Decision,* 34(9), Special Issue on "Strategic Management in the Asia Pacific," pp. 21–33.

Haley, U. C. V., and F.-J. Richter (2002), *Asian Post-Crisis Management. Corporate and Governmental Strategies for Sustainable Competitive Advantage*, New York: Palgrave.

Haley, U. C. V., and S. A. Stumpf (1989), "Cognitive Trails in Strategic Decision-Making: Linking Theories of Personalities and Cognitions," *Journal of Management Studies*, Vol. 26(5), pp. 477–497.

Hall, J. W., and J. G. Kirk (eds.) (1988), *History of the World*, Greenwich, CT: Bison Books.

Hamilton, G. G. (1996), "The Theoretical Significance of Asian Business Networks," in G. G. Hamilton (ed.), *Asian Business Networks*, Berlin, New York: Walter de Gruyter, pp. 283–298.

Hamilton, G. G. (1997), "Organization and Market Process in Taiwan's Capitalistic Economy," in M. Orrú, N. W. Biggart, and G. G. Hamilton (eds.), *The Economic Organization of East Asian Capitalism*, Thousand Oaks, CA, New Delhi, London: Sage, pp. 237–296.

Hamilton, G. G., and W. Zheng (1992), "Introduction: Fei Xiaotong and the Beginnings of Chinese Sociology," in X. Fei (1992), *From the Soil: The Foundation of Chinese Society*, Berkeley: University of California Press, pp. 1–34.

Heilbroner, R. L., and A. Singer (1984), *The Economic Transformation of America: 1600 to the Present*, 2nd edition, New York: Harcourt Brace Jovanovich.

Hofer, C. W., and D. Schendel (1978), *Strategy Formulation: Analytical Concepts*, St. Paul, MN: West.

Hofstede, G. (1994), "Cultural Constraints in Management Theories," *International Review of Strategic Management*, Vol. 5, D. E. Hussey (ed.), West Sussex, UK: John Wiley & Sons, pp. 27–47.

Khanna, T., and K. Palepu (July/August 1997), "Why Focused Strategies May Be Wrong for Emerging Markets," *Harvard Business Review*.

Kohut, J., and A. T. Cheng (March 1996), "Return of the Merchant Mandarins," *Asia, Inc.*, pp. 22–31.

Kraar, L., and W. Woods (March 4, 1996). "Need a Friend in Asia? Try the Singapore Connection: Good News for Multi-National Companies. Their Most Trusted Partner in the Far East Is Making Copies of Itself in China, India, Indonesia, and Vietnam." *Fortune*.

Kristof, N. D. (January 17, 1998), "Crisis Pushing Asian Capitalism Closer to U.S.-Style Free Market," *New York Times*.

Lau, D. C. (1963), *Lao Tzu: Tao Te Ching*, London: Penguin Books.

Lau, D. C. (1995), *Mencius Says*, Singapore: Federal Publications, Pte. Ltd.

Lee, S. H., and P. H. Phan (2006), "The Effects of Tie Strength and Tie Diversity on Job Search, Pay Increases, and Promotion in Singapore and Thailand," *Journal of Social and Personal Relationships*, Vol. 23(5), pp. 820–839.

Legge, J. (1970), *The Works of Mencius*, New York: Cover Publications.

Loh, G., C. B. Goh, and T. L. Tan (2000), *Building Bridges, Carving Niches: An Enduring Legacy*, Singapore: Oxford University Press.

Maynard, M. (November 14, 2007), "Better Cars, Worse Sales." *New York Times*, pp. C1 and C9.

Mintzberg, H. (July/August 1987), "Crafting Strategy," *Harvard Business Review*, pp. 66–75.

Mintzberg, H. (January/February 1994), "The Fall and Rise of Strategic Planning," *Harvard Business Review*, pp. 107–114.

Mintzberg, H., and J. Waters (1985), "Of Strategies, Deliberate and Emergent," *Strategic Management Journal*, no. 6, pp. 257–272.

Mizruchi, M. S., and M. Schwartz (1987), *Intercorporate Relations: The Structural Analysis of Business*, Cambridge, UK: Cambridge University Press.

Nakamura, G. I. (1992), "Development of Strategic Management in the Asia Pacific Region," in D. E. Hussey (ed.), *International Review of Strategic Management*, Vol. 3, John Wiley & Sons, West Sussex, pp. 3–18.

Nanto, D. K. (February 6, 1998), "The 1997–98 Asian Financial Crisis," Congressional Research Service.

Neupert, K. E., C. C. Baughn, and T.T.L. Dao (2005), "International Management Skills for Success in Asia: A Needs-Based Determination of Skills for Foreign Managers and Local Managers," *Journal of European Industrial Training*, Vol. 39(2), pp. 165–180.

Nissen, M. E. (2006), *Harnessing Knowledge Dynamics: Principled Organization Knowing and Learning*, Hershey, PA: IRM Press.

Nohria, N., and R. G. Eccles (1992), *Networks and Organizations: Structure, Form and Action*, Cambridge, MA: Harvard Business School Press.

Nonaka, I., and H. Takeuchi (1995), *The Knowledge-Creating Company: How Japanese Companies Create the Dynamics of Innovation*, New York: Oxford University Press.

Ohmae, K. (1990), *The Borderless World: Power, Strategy in the Interlinked Economy*, New York: HarperCollins.

Polanyi, M. (1959), *The Study of Man*, Chicago: University of Chicago Press.

Polanyi, M. (1962), *Personal Knowledge: Toward a Postcritical Philosophy*, Chicago: University of Chicago Press.

Polanyi, M. (1966), *The Tacit Dimension*, Garden City, NY: Doubleday.

Polanyi, M. (1969), *Knowing and Being: Essays by Michael Polanyi*, London: Routledge & Kegan Paul.

Prahalad, C. K. and G. Hamel (May/June 1990), "The Core Competence of the Corporation," *Harvard Business Review*, pp. 79–91.

Redding, S. G. (1986), "Entrepreneurship in Asia," *Euro-Asia Business Review*, Vol. 5(4), pp. 23–27.

Redding, S. G. (1993), *The Spirit of Chinese Capitalism*, New York: de Gruyter.

Redding, S. G. (1995), "Overseas Chinese Networks: Understanding the Enigma," *Long Range Planning*, Vol. 28(1), pp. 61–69.

Redding, S. G. (1996), "Weak Organization and Strong Linkages: Managerial Ideology and Chinese Family Business Networks," in G. G. Hamilton (ed.), *Asian Business Networks*, Berlin, New York: Walter de Gruyter, pp. 27–42.

Redding, S. G., and M. Hsiao (1993), "An Empirical Study of Overseas Chinese Ideology," in P. Blunt and D. Richards (eds.), *Readings in Management, Organization and Culture in East and South-East Asia*, Darwin, Australia: NTU Press, pp. 174–184.

Robertson, J. (2003), "The Economic Cost of Infectious Diseases," Research Note 36 2002–03, *Foreign Affairs*, Defense and Trade Group, Parliament of Australia.

Rodan, G. (June 21, 2007), "Scrutinizing Singapore." *Wall Street Journal*.

Siu, A., and Y. C. R. Wong (2005), "Counting the Cost: The Economic and Social Cost of SARS," in M. Peiris, *Severe Acute Respiratory Syndrome, a Clinical Guide*, Oxford: Wiley-Blackwell.

Slywotsky, A. J., and B. P. Shapiro (September/October 1993), "Leveraging to Beat the Odds: The New Marketing Mind-Set," *Harvard Business Review*, pp. 97–107.

Strachan, H. (1976), *Families and Other Business Groups in Business Development: The Case of Nicaragua*, New York: Praeger.

Studwell, J. (2007), *Asian Godfathers: Money and Power in Hong Kong and Southeast Asia*, New York: Atlantic Monthly Press.

Tan, S. U. (1991), *Letters from Thailand*, Bangkok, Thailand: Editions Duang Kamol.

Tanzer, A. (July 28, 1997), "The Amazing Mr. Kuok," *Forbes*, 90–95.

The Economist (March 9–15, 1996), "The Limits of Family Values," in a special "Survey of Business in Asia," pp. 12–22.

The Economist (April 7–13, 2001), "From Bamboo to Bits and Bytes," in a special "Survey of Asian Business," p. 8.

The Economist (November 9, 2007), "Gold from the Storm," June 28, Web version.

The Economist (February 28, 2008), "The Tigers That Lost Their Roar."

Tsui-Auch, L. S. (2006), "Singaporean Business Groups: The Role of the State and Capital in Singapore Inc." In S.-J. Chang (ed.),

Business Groups in East Asia: Financial Crisis, Restructuring and New Growth (pp. 94–115). Oxford, UK: Oxford University Press.

Tucker, S. (November 27, 2007), "Not-so-Instant Exposure," *Financial Times*, Special Report on Property, p. 8.

Vatikiotis, M. (February 26, 1998), "The Chinese Way," *Far Eastern Economic Review*, p. 45.

Vatikiotis, M. (November 26, 2004), "Indonesian Food Giant Undergoes a Transformation," *New York Times*.

Vatikiotis, M., and P. Daorueng (February 26, 1998), "Survival Tactics," *Far Eastern Economic Review*, pp. 42–45.

Wada, K. (1992), *Yaohan's Global Strategy, the 21st Century Is the Era of Asia*, Hong Kong: Capital Communications.

Waley, A. (1996), *Confucius: The Analects*, Ware, Hertfordshire, UK: Wordsworth Editions.

Wang G. (1991), *China and the Chinese Overseas*, Singapore: Times Academic Press.

Whitley, R. (1992), *Business Systems in East Asia: Firms, Markets and Societies*, London: Sage.

Whitley, R. (1999), *Divergent Capitalisms: The Social Structuring and Change of Business Systems*, Oxford: Oxford University Press.

Whitley, R. (2008), *Business Systems and Organizational Capabilities: The Institutional Structuring of Competitive Competences*, Oxford: Oxford University Press.

Yamashita, S. (1991), "Japan's Role as a Regional Technological Integrator in the Pacific Rim," paper presented at the Conference on the Emerging Technological Trajectory of the Pacific Rim, Tufts University, Medford, MA, Oct. 4–6.

Yeo, V. (April 14, 2008), "Asian Businesses Get Ready for Data Explosion," *BusinessWeek*.

Yong, C. F. (1987), *A Short Biography of Tan Kah Kee*, Singapore: Tan Kah Kee Foundation.

Young, S. B. (July 12, 2002), "Family Businesses and Reforms in Corporate Governance," Caux Round Table, Institute of Policy Studies, Singapore.

Zang, X. (1999), "Research Note: Personalism and Corporate Networks in Singapore," *Organization Studies*, pp. 861–877.

In addition to the bibliography, countless articles in these publications have provided background and depth:

Asia, Inc.	*www.asia-inc.com/*
Asian Business	*www.cgi.cnn.com/ASIANOW/asiaweek/*
AsiaWeek	*www.apmforum.com/*
The Australian	*www.theaustralian.news.com.au/*
Business Times (of Singapore)	*www.businesstimes.com.sg/*
Business Week	*www.businessweek.com/*
The Economist	*www.economist.com/*
Far Eastern Economic Review	*www.feer.com/*
Financial Times	*www.ft.com/home/us*
Forbes	*www.forbes.com/*
Fortune	*www.money.cnn.com/magazines/fortune/*
International Herald Tribune	*www.iht.com/*
Los Angeles Times	*www.latimes.com/*
New York Times	*www.nytimes.com/*
Newsweek	*www.newsweek.com/*
Next (of Hong Kong)	*www.next.atnext.com/chineselanguage*
The Straits Times (of Singapore)	*www.straitstimes.com/*
Time	*www.time.com/time/*

List of Interviewees

Note: The interviews took place over a decade from 1997 to 2008, before and after the Asian financial crisis and SARS. This list is incomplete because some of the New Asian Emperors with whom we spoke requested anonymity.

Steven Chan, formerly executive chairman, Superior Multi-Packaging, Ltd.

Justin Chiu, executive director, Cheung Kong Holdings

Victor Fung, executive chairman, Li & Fung Group (*world's largest trading company*)

Goh Cheng Liang, founder, Wuthelam Group

Goh Hup Jin, CEO, Wuthelam Group

Kwek Leng Beng, executive chairman, Hong Leong Group

Butt Lau, director, Li & Fung Group

Li Ka-shing, chairman, Cheung Kong Holdings and Hutchison Whampoa (*Hong Kong's richest man, and 11th-richest individual on Forbes 2008 list of the world's billionaires*)

(Mrs.) Lim Siew Hua, chairwoman, Sateri International Group (an RGM International Group company)

Philip Ng, executive director and CEO, Far East Organization, Singapore

Stephen Riady, president, Lippo Group

Stan Shih, founder and chairman, Acer Inc.

Sukanto Tanoto, founder, RGM International (*Indonesia's richest man, and 284th richest individual on Forbes 2008 list of the world's billionaires*)

Thio Gim Hock, CEO and group managing director, Overseas Union Enterprise, Ltd.

Wee Cho Yaw, chairman, United Overseas Bank (*Singapore's second richest man, and 396th richest individual on Forbes 2008 list of the world's billionaires*)

Wee Ee Cheong, deputy chairman and CEO, United Overseas Bank

Other CEOs and Senior Executives

Note: Again, an incomplete list, interviewed over a period of a decade from 1994 to 2008.

Arnold Alderman, president, Anagenesis, Inc.

Sam Bergami, CEO, Alinabal Corp.

Rick Schart, vice president of transportation, JCPenney Corp.

Lorenzo Zambrano, CEO, CEMEX

Edward Zeng, founder and CEO, Sparkice (China)